Praise for

The Self Confidence & Self Esteem Bible
by Sarah PJ White

"SAY GOODBYE TO YOUR EXCUSES. Possibly the most concise self-help book I've ever read! Be prepared to have every "yeah-but" quashed as Sarah takes on anything and everything that stands between you and your self-confidence. This is a book you'll want to refer back to again and again and again."
– Peter Jones, author of
How To Do Everything and Be Happy
http://howtodoeverythingandbehappy.com

"I believe *'The Self Confidence & Self Esteem Bible'* is a good starting resource for women who wish to improve their self confidence and/or self esteem."
– Dr Joe Vitale, #1 bestselling author of
'The Attractor Factor'
www.mrfire.com

"As a mum I am very aware how easy it is for women to lose touch with themselves whilst fulfilling the role of wife and mother. Having held down a large job in my twenties, the 5 years I took out of work to bring up my three children sent me spinning at the thought of being back in a Boardroom, or standing presenting in front of people. It took very little time to lose the confidence and re-building it was critical for my role as a mother and for my marriage to maintain its zest. *The Self Confidence & Self Esteem Bible'* is a good starting resource for those wishing to reconnect with themselves again, find themselves and be a person in their own right."

– Penny Power, founder of
Ecademy and Digital Youth Academy
www.twitter.com/pennypower

"Over the last 15 years, having worked with hundreds of coaching clients, first as a wealth coach and founder of The Money Gym, then as an online business success mentor, I've noticed more and more that financial success in particular is never about how clever someone is, or how technically skilled they are, it's always about their ability to take action and feel confidence about overcoming obstacles. If you are not yet as successful as you would like to be, this book is a straightforward and practical guide to going straight to the root of your problem and working out how to fix it. Essential reading!"

– Nicola Cairncross
Author, Speaker, Entrepreneur
http://TheBusinessSuccessFactory.com

"What a valuable and powerful read! As a busy mum and full time business owner, I can fully relate to the stresses and strains that women endure and believe this book to be exactly what the title states *'The Self Confidence & Self Esteem Bible'*."

– Alison Crook
Pink Whizz Promotions
www.pinkwhizzpromotions.co.uk

THE SELF CONFIDENCE
&
SELF ESTEEM BIBLE

The one-stop resource for stressed wives & mothers on understanding, building & keeping your self confidence and self esteem

SARAH PJ WHITE

WHITE HEART PUBLISHING
Berkshire, United Kingdom

WHITE HEART PUBLISHING

Copyright © Sarah PJ White 2012

Published 2012, in Great Britain,
by White Heart Publishing
www.whiteheartpublishing.co.uk

All rights reserved. No part of this publication may be reproduced, stored in a retrieval system, or transmitted in any form or by any means, electronic, mechanical, photocopy, recording or otherwise, without prior written permission of the copyright owner. Nor can it be circulated in any form of binding or cover other than that in which it is published and without similar condition including this condition being imposed on a subsequent purchaser.

Please visit **www.whiteheartpublishing.co.uk**
for contact details.

ISBN 978-0-9573679-0-6

British Cataloguing Publication Data:
A catalogue record of this book is available from the British Library

This book is also available as an eBook, for your kindle, nook etc...

Disclaimer:

This book is intended to be a general introduction, to assist those people who would like to improve their self confidence and self esteem. The information within this book is neither comprehensive nor prescriptive, and the advice does not address individual circumstances and conditions. The author (and publisher) is not medically trained and the information within the pages of this Book is not intended to substitute a visit to your local GP if you are feeling abnormally depressed or low. If in any doubt, always consult a Doctor.

*Dedicated to Phyllis Mallows,
a nan who inspired an entire generation
to be whatever they wanted.*

Phyllis Ruby Mallows (nee Harris & Underhill)
13/01/1922 – 17/02/2010

Contents

FOREWORD by Curly Martin xiii
INTRODUCTION 1

SECTION 1 – COMMON QUESTIONS 11
QUESTION 1: What is Low Self Esteem? 13
What Are The Symptoms & Results of Low Self Esteem? 14
What Are The End Results? 17
QUESTION 2: What is Low Self Confidence? 19
What Are The Symptoms & Results of Low Self Confidence? ... 20
What Are The End Results? 22
QUESTION 3: What Causes Low Self Confidence & Esteem? .. 25
QUESTION 4: What is Anxiety & How Do You Overcome it? .. 31
What Are The Symptoms of Anxiety? 31
How Does Anxiety Affect You? 32
What Causes Anxiety? 33
How Do You Solve An Anxiety Problem? 33
QUESTION 5: Why Do I Feel So Low? 35
What Symptoms Are There? 35
How Will Feeing So Low Affect You? 36
What Causes Me To Feel So Low? 37
How Do I Solve This Problem? 38
QUESTION 6: Why Am I Unhappy? 41
What symptoms Are There? 41
How Will Feeing So Unhappy Affect You? 42
What Causes Me To Feel So Unhappy? 43
How Do I Solve This Problem of Unhappiness? 46
QUESTION 7: Why Am I Ugly? 49
The Symptoms & End Results of Holding This Belief 50
What Causes Me To Hold This Belief About Myself? 51
How Do I Solve The Problem of Having This Belief? 52
QUESTION 8: Why Do I Feel Like A Failure? 55
What Symptoms Are There For This Belief? 56
What Causes Me To Feel This Way? 56
How Do I Solve The Problem of This Negative Belief? 59

QUESTION 9: What Do I Really Want? 61
How Can I Improve My Chances? 63
QUESTION 10: How Do You Stay Positive? 65
Possible Causes For Struggling With Positivity 66
Steps To Help You Stay Positive 67
BONUS QUESTION 11: Where Do You Find Happiness? 69

SECTION 2 – ASSESSING YOUR CURRENT SITUATION 73
CHAPTER 12: Rating Your Current Situation 75
CHAPTER 13: The Core Beliefs You Live By 81
What is your belief structure? 81
How Beliefs are Made 82
How We Use Beliefs 83
Limiting Beliefs 84
CHAPTER 14: Our Self Talk 85
The Power of Words 85
Self Talk 86
Negative Inner Talk 87
CHAPTER 15: Your Emotions 89
What Are Emotions? 89
How Emotions Affect You 90
How We Learn To Associate Our Memories 91
The Negative Emotions That Can Stop You In Your Tracks 92
CHAPTER 16: The Stress In Your Life 95
What is Stress? 95
How Stress Affects You 96
CHAPTER 17: Facing Your Fears 99
Fear is Natural 99
How We Get Them? 100
How Do Fears Affect Us? 101
The Big Fears 101

SECTION 3 – MOVING FORWARD; SOLVING THOSE
PROBLEMS RELATED TO LOW SELF CONFIDENCE AND
SELF ESTEEM 105
CHAPTER 18: Moving Forward 107
Important Things to Remember 108
CHAPTER 19: Goal Setting & Motivation 115

Basics of Goal Setting 115
Staying Motivated 120
Possible Causes For Struggling With Motivation 120
Steps To Help You Stay Motivated 122
CHAPTER 20: Action Stations! 125
Compiling your Action Plan 125
CHAPTER 21: Sorting Those Gremlins That Hold You Back .. 133
How To Change Your Beliefs.. 133
How To Change Your Thoughts 135
How To Get A Handle On Your Emotions................................. 138
How To Manage Stress 140
How To Solve Your Fears 145

SECTION 4 – TOOLS IN YOUR ARSENAL............................... 149
CHAPTER 22: Affirmations & Positivity Quotes 151
What is an Affirmation? 151
How To Use Affirmations... 152
What are positivity quotes and what are they used for?........... 153
How to use positivity quotes 153
CHAPTER 23: Visualisation & Vision Boards.......................... 155
What is visualisation?... 155
How to use visualisation... 156
What are vision boards? 158
CHAPTER 24: Gratitude & Gratitude Journals 161
What is Gratitude?.. 161
Why use gratitude? 162
Things that stop you showing gratitude 164
Ways to use gratitude in your life 164
Gratitude journal 166
How to use a gratitude journal... 166

SECTION 5 – FURTHER HELP AND AVAILABLE
RESOURCES.. 171
FURTHER HELP AND CONTACT INFORMATION 173
Books Worth Getting 173
Websites to Mark as Favourites 173

FOREWORD by Curly Martin

I first met Sarah when she attended one of my Life Coaching Diploma courses way back in October 2006, where she started her studies to become a life coach. She completed her training and qualified a year later and since this time she has used and adapted the techniques and models to great effect, some of which she has incorporated into this packed book.

Sarah has pulled together her personal experience, knowledge, research and learning into a highly focussed, easy to follow resource on confidence and self esteem, with particular emphasis on helping stressed wives and mothers. Although Sarah compiled the book with stressed wives and mothers in mind, its appeal will go way beyond this group. It will prove an invaluable help to anyone who is struggling with questions such as, 'Why do I feel like a failure?' and 'How do I stay positive?'

Sarah has cleverly divided the book into a natural progression of five sections which guide the reader from self enquiry, through to further help and resources. At the beginning she gives clear and concise reasons for why you should read what she has to say and who should be reading this book.

She starts and concludes each chapter with interesting and relevant quotes from Andrew Carnegie to Zig Ziglar, which add extra contemplation and depth. The book covers the situations where women can find themselves doubting their abilities, questioning their rights, feeling anxious and unworthy, which in turn lower self esteem and impact on confidence levels. The book then goes on to offer the reader a variety of solutions to explore, including self-talk, visualisation, affirmations, facing fear, goal setting and gratitude.

I wish Sarah and her readers ever increasing confidence, success and happiness.

– Curly Martin
International Bestselling Author
www.curlymartin.com

INTRODUCTION

Why This Book Has Been Written

As women we spend our lives frequently doing what others want us to do, often out of a sense of duty. We often feel unhappy without necessarily knowing why we are so unhappy with 'our lot'. Out of the two sexes, women in particular, spend their time being who they feel they 'should be', acting how they think they 'should act', and making sure everyone around them is happy – regardless of how they feel inside.

We are brilliant at tending to others. As children we are bought up to help our parents and siblings. We get older and start relationships, based on keeping the other person happy then we have children and devote our lives to ensuring they are happy, healthy and are living to their potential.

We look after those around us, catering for their emotional and physical needs. We keep the house and garden tidy, make sure everyone is fed and watered – often including the household pets too! We employ our time-management skills to ensure everybody is where they should be, when then should be – and will quite often drop what we're doing to be the household taxi driver too.

We nurse our partners and children (and often – our parents) when they are sick or injured. We cater to their emotional needs too – offering a shoulder to cry on for our family and friends, comforting words of support or sympathy when needed. We fight battles for our nearest and dearest and one of our chief aims is to ensure everyone is healthy, happy, safe and loved.

We run around doing all this without a second thought for ourselves. Yet, in our rare quiet times, we are yearning for a bit of peace and quiet; just wishing that occasionally the roundabout will stop so we can catch our breath and remember what we want – who we want to be and what we want to do. We long to feel supported and loved – you see, we already feel needed, but sometimes, the fact that so many people want a piece of us, can be quite suffocating. We feel we want to be needed for who we are – not what we do.

We get so caught up with rushing around for others – we can sometimes lose sight of ourselves. We feel unhappy and sad; heavy and deflated. We can sometimes feel like a non-person; we don't exist for, or as ourselves. In our busy lives we easily sweep our true feelings and dreams under the carpet, causing our energy to dim, our dreams and wishes diminish and our heart gets heavy.

Regardless of where you are right now, I can help you feel happier with your life and, more importantly, happy with yourself. I can help you feel like each day is a shining opportunity for you to be who you want to be, where you wake up full of energy and confidence. A time when you can look in the mirror and see an amazing woman staring back at you with love and pride reflected in her eyes. I can gently guide you forward, towards a time when you are loved and appreciated by those around you; where you feel loved and supported – by your friends, family and yourself –even if you don't believe it is possible at the moment.

I would love for you to experience a life of happiness, confidence and opportunity. Where each day is greeted as a bright new opportunity; full of potential – rather than waking with a feeling of dread. I hope you find the inspiration that you crave and the inspiration to start your journey, right here and right now.

Why Should You Listen to Me?

I am a qualified life coach, author, freelance writer and above all else – a wife and mother! I have suffered from low self esteem and confidence and know how it can impact on your life. I know how unhappy, lonely and disconnected it can make you feel. I know what it's like to cry yourself to sleep at night, thinking you are unloved, unwanted and hating yourself for it. I've seen first-hand the impact it has on your relationships – both on the good ones and bad ones. I've been on the receiving end of verbal and sexual abuse and had my esteem and confidence at an almost non-existent level – and I've come out the other side as a better person.

I'm now married to a wonderful man, have my own teenage daughter, step-daughters and an extended family. I've seen both sides of the coin – raising a child on your own and integrating with another family. I've seen how having the love and support of yourself and others can raise you to new heights and propel you forward.

I'm not here to tell you how 'perfect' my life is; nor am I going to tell you my confidence and esteem levels never dip down – because that would be untrue and make me a liar. What I am here to tell you is working on your self confidence and esteem is always going to be a work in progress – a lifelong commitment. What makes it easier however, is knowing that your 'work in progress' is a lot easier and quicker to deal with when you know what you're dealing with and where you are headed. I can tell you that it gets easier to spot (and deal with) issues before they become problems and the 'ups' will become far more frequent and outweigh the 'downs' (that will lessen and be less significant).

My ambition is to help empower women and enable them to be happy in their own skin, full of self confidence and with a healthy esteem for themselves. I focus my work on helping wives, mothers and women in general, get the very best they can out of their lives in a creative, gentle and inspiring way.

This book is an introduction for you to use; a resource to begin your journey into better self confidence and self esteem. It more than just another book – it is a complete course on building your self confidence and self esteem. It is part of my ongoing online project at Self Confidence Workshops – a practical, self improvement portal designed to give you a one-stop place to access free articles and resources, along with low fee courses - in an effort to provide you with a one-stop resource for all you may need to improve your self confidence and self esteem.

Who Is this Book For?

Any person can use this book as a resource for building their confidence and esteem, however it has been predominantly written to relate to women who class themselves as one or more of the following:

- A wife or partner
- Mother
- feels stressed and uptight
- Unhappy with life and the life they are currently living
- feels unsupported, lonely and isolated
- Frustrated
- Unsure of who they are
- Aware they are repeating negative patterns in their life but unsure why
- Unhappy with themselves as a person (appearance and/or attitude)
- Feels like they are living the wrong life
- Feels like they have missed their chance in life

How to Use This Book

This book has been written to give you the first steps in improving and keeping your self confidence and self esteem. You are about to start an incredible, inspiring, life changing journey, so I wanted you to have a single port of reference to make those first steps easier for you.

Within these pages you will find some of the most commonly asked questions people have about confidence and self esteem. Knowing the answer – and having a solution (or action plan) to make the answers relate to you, in your individual circumstances – is the key to helping you move forward. It is full of inspiring quotes to keep you in a positive mindset as well as practical exercises and tips to help you start building and boosting your confidence and esteem.

What Does This Mean For You?

I am giving you the opportunity to take my hand and let me lead you through those first steps to better self confidence and esteem. Taking those first steps will enable you to:

- Feel guided and supported
- Let go of those feelings of frustration
- Overcome feelings of hopelessness, loneliness and isolation
- Take steps to reconnect with you – reconnect with your goals and dreams
- Be inspired towards living the life you were meant to live

What This Book Covers:

You know you want to move forward; develop your self esteem to a healthier level and boost your confidence, but you probably have lots of questions. Sometimes you may feel that the answers are obvious – but knowing and acting on what you know are two different things.

This book is divided into five sections, with inspiring quotes (to keep you motivated and in a positive frame of mind) sprinkled throughout. The information within the pages of this Book is divided up as follows:

Section 1:

This section will cover 10 commonly asked questions about self confidence and self esteem, along with corresponding answers to those questions

Section 2:

Is all about assessing your current position and circumstances, along with how you feel about it. You cannot move forward until you understand your starting position, so in this section we learn about our core beliefs, self talk and inner speech patterns along with the stress and fears you currently have. We look at emotions and how we link all these areas together.

Section 3:

Now you have assessed your current position we will look at building a personalised plan of action steps that can take you from where you are to where you want to be.

Section 4:

Section 4 is all about giving you an insight into those extra tools you can utilise to help you move forward, as well as keeping you where you want to be. We cover affirmations, visualisation and vision boards, along with positive quotes and using gratitude to keep your focus on the good in your life.

Section 5:
This section is all about further resources, including links to the templates (for use with this book), details for contacting the author and further help available to you through our online courses

Working on your self confidence and self esteem is a rather in depth theme, covering a wide range of topics, some of which I can only hope to touch the surface of with this Book. It touches upon the subjects of goal setting and motivation, however to get a more in-depth look at these subjects you would need to look into dedicated courses and books to really cover them in any great detail.

What I hope you will get from this Book, is an insight into these areas, enabling you to narrow down those that do need your attention; allowing you to either look at them in greater detail with a dedicated course, or to examine all those areas a bit more, with a self confidence and self esteem course.

"I wish I could show you, when you are lonely or in darkness,
the astonishing Light of your own Being."
– Hafiz

SECTION 1 – COMMON QUESTIONS

In this section, we will be looking at the ten most commonly asked questions, relating to self confidence and self esteem.

Each individual question is given its own chapter (some bonus directly related questions are also answered, if relevant) and a comprehensive answer is broken down in the paragraphs that follow. The questions start off with a more general approach; giving an overview of low self confidence and low esteem, before targeting on more specific issues.

These questions serve as a useful aid to establishing how you feel and what you believe. This will enable you to use the information in the subsequent chapters for creating a complete picture of where you currently are, along with a more targeted plan of action to get you where you want to be.

To get the most out of this chapter, whilst reading the following questions, keep a pen handy, and write down any thoughts and emotions that crop up. If any of the specific questions ring true for you, spend 5-10 minutes to think about what that means to you; how it makes you feel, how it affects you etc.

This first section can be quite tough, as it can stir up a lot of emotions, but stick with it, as your answers and insights will give you a useful head start for the subsequent sections in this book. So, without further ado, let's move on to the questions!

QUESTION 1

*"Persons of high self-esteem are not driven to make themselves superior to others;
They do not seek to prove their value by measuring themselves against a comparative standard. Their joy is being who they are, not in being better than someone else"*

- Nathaniel Branden

What is Low Self Esteem?

Self esteem is how you feel about yourself. It can grow and expand or contract and wither – a bit like a plant. A plant needs certain things to enable it to grow. These include soil, light and water, to enable it to flourish, grow and flower.

Our esteem is like a plant, it needs certain things to make it blossom too. These include -

- happiness
- health
- love
- joy
- forgiveness
- success
- life

Having low self esteem is when you feel bad about you as a person. However, it is so much more than just feeling bad about yourself. Having low self esteem means that you also feel unworthy. Quite often, low self esteem means you feel unworthy of having any (or all) of the things listed above).

What Are The Symptoms & Results of Low Self Esteem?

Low self esteem can show up in a variety of ways, depending on what type of person you are and what type of lifestyle you lead.

Sabotage & Confirmation

As a person who suffers from low esteem, you will sabotage certain (or even all) areas of your life. Predominantly you will attack the area you feel most unworthy of and as your esteem falls lower, it will have a domino effect on your life, as one area effects another, so you will move on to sabotaging the other areas in your life. This is born from a need to look for ways to confirm that your decision to dislike yourself is correct. For example:

- If you believe you are not worthy of love, you will sabotage (consciously or subconsciously) any relationships you have – whether they are with family or partners, by cheating, pushing close people away or generally behaving in a way that will eventually drive the other person away. You may stay with a violent or toxic partner or even be the violent or toxic person yourself.
- If you believe you are not worthy of good health, or even your life in general, you will go out of your way to sabotage these areas of your life. You may put yourself in dangerous jobs or unsafe positions and areas; you

may take drugs or practice unprotected and/or casual sex.

Acting Like A Doormat

As a person who doesn't think very much of yourself, you will allow others to treat you as you see fit. Unfortunately, much too often, this means allowing other people to walk over you. All too often you may put your own needs at the back of the ever-increasing queue of other people's demands.

You will run around after everyone else, being at their beck and call because, let's face it – that's all you think you are worth. If you think you are only fit to be a skivvy, or you think you are worthless and deserve negative comments and verbal abuse or – even worse – a punch bag, then that is how others will treat you.

You allow others to talk down to you and use negative words to describe you or belittle you. You will allow others to treat you as they see fit. They can shout or scream at you, hit you and bad mouth you, but you will stay silent, as on the inside, you believe it this is what you deserve.

Life is Pointless/Life is a Battlefield/Life is Against Us

Often we will see life as a big struggle. Life conspires against us. Because of how we treat ourselves, and how others treat us, we feel that our needs and wants just aren't important. We feel that like takes great joy in making us look like the court jester.

Negative Speech Patterns

Your low self esteem will also show up in the way you talk about yourself. The most popular phrases that will come out of your mouth will include:

- I'm sorry
- I'm so stupid/dumb etc

- I'm useless
- Why am I so pathetic, weak, feeble etc
- I'm fine, don't worry about me (or don't worry about it)
- I look a mess

You will constantly put yourself down. If someone pays you a compliment, you will quite often tell them not to be silly, or brush off the compliment with a negative ('oh, this old thing?' or 'it didn't cost very much at all' and even 'you're just saying that to be nice').

Often, you tend to beat yourself up over the smallest of errors. You may drop and smash a mug; but you will use it to confirm to yourself that you are an idiot, stupid, clumsy, etc and quite often you will tell others about it so they can confirm how bad you are too!

Negative Inner Talk

This is the only area of low self esteem that other people cannot see. It is also one of the most destructive of symptoms, as we often don't notice it running riot inside our mind.

A lot of the phrases mentioned under 'negative speech patterns' apply in this section too, however they are far more destructive when not uttered out loud. The reason for this is because they can be repeated over and over again. Often, this is become such a habit to us, we no longer hear it or notice it.

Your brain has a staggering average 70,000 thoughts a day – with an approximate 80% of those being negative. That's an **incredible average amount of 56,000 negative thoughts a day!** You cannot hope to be consciously aware of that amount of thought each day, so the vast majority of those thoughts are left to run riot in your mind, rooting and confirming those negative thought patterns further inside your brain, the more you confirm they are true.

What Are The End Results?

A person with low self esteem will be left feeling:

- frightened and vulnerable
- fearful
- stressed and tense
- stagnant, no energy spirit is trapped – no sense of connection

They will also have:

- closed their mind to new possibilities
- weak personal power
- no defence against challenges life may throw their way

What Causes Low Self Esteem and How Can I Solve It?

Before I answer that question, there is another related area we have to address – self confidence, as low self esteem will often have a knock-on effect on your confidence (this is covered in Chapter 2).

"You yourself, as much as anybody in the entire universe,
deserve your love and affection."

– Buddha

QUESTION 2

*"We do not believe in ourselves until someone reveals
that deep inside us something is valuable, worth
listening to, worthy of our trust, sacred to our touch.
Once we believe
in ourselves we can risk curiosity, wonder, spontaneous
delight or any experience
that reveals the human spirit."*

– E E Cummings

What is Low Self Confidence?

We've already established that self esteem is how you feel about yourself; how much you think you are worth. Self confidence is how much faith you have in your own judgements, abilities and power.

It is often linked to self esteem, as they both play a part in how you present yourself to the outside world. Let's face it; if you don't think very highly of yourself as a person, you aren't really going to have a lot of confidence in what you do.

Your confidence can also vary depending on your environment. For example, at home you may feel more confident than you do at work, or vice versa.

What Are The Symptoms and Results of Low Self Confidence?

Low self confidence can show up in a variety of ways, depending on the environment you are in and the people you are with. It doesn't always go hand-in-hand with low self esteem. You might be a person who actually has quite a healthy self image, but don't have much faith in your abilities.

Some of the symptoms of low self confidence are listed below. Again, it is worth reiterating, these symptoms will show up in the areas you aren't confident in. You may be the life and soul at a party, but your lack of confidence may be in a work-related environment.

So, some of the symptoms of low self confidence include:

Lack of Effort

You may have the mentality of 'I'm not going to be very good at this, so I won't even try'. Obviously, if you also suffer from low self esteem, this in one of the areas you may be sabotaging yourself excessively in. If you aren't confident in your ability and already consider yourself a failure – how much effort will you actually be willing to put into failing?

Trust in Others/Outside Factors

You will look for confirmation from other people, in an effort to confirm your inabilities. You will be an expert at pointing out that other people are far more suited to the job at hand. You also firmly believe that putting your trust in that other person is a safer bet than trusting yourself.

Outside factors are useful in contributing to a suitable excuse. You may not be wearing suitable clothes, the weather may not be right, or you have loads of ironing/dusting/hair-washing to do. Basically, any other job may suddenly become more appealing than dealing with what's in front of you.

Shyness/Embarrassment

If your confidence is low, you may find it easier to hide behind your developed shyness. You'll be the person at the party who is trying desperately to blend in with the wallpaper, rather than talk to people you don't know.

Shyness often has embarrassment at the root of it. You would rather stay quiet and timid, as it's often easier than risking putting yourself forward and risking being embarrassed in any way.

Feelings/Emotional

As a person who has low confidence, you may be overly sensitive to your feelings and emotions. You're more sensitive to what other people say about you, as you're always on the lookout for confirmation that you were right to doubt yourself.

The trouble with this is, often it is a double-edge sword. You want the confirmation that you are correct to doubt yourself, but you will tend to be upset over hearing that confirmation.

Procrastinating

If you doubt your abilities, power and judgement, you will put off moving forward. For example:

- if you doubt your abilities at work, you may put off dealing with a customer or compiling a report etc. You'll probably leave it to the last minute, or not complete it at all
- if you're unsure of your judgement in relationships, you may delay going on that girl's night out or put off calling that number you've been handed by a potential partner.

Assertiveness

Your lack of confidence means you won't be putting yourself forward in your area of concern as you won't be very assertive. You also won't want to have your say – you'd rather keep quiet, otherwise you may draw attention to yourself and risk being put forward for whatever you are trying to avoid.

Social network

Your social network will play a part in your lack of confidence. As the saying goes: 'like attracts like'. Look at the people you hang around with. The chances are you have picked other people who are equally low in confidence. You may also hang around with someone who is really assertive and confident, so you can play at hiding in their shadow.

Health issues/problems

Sometimes a lack of confidence is linked to you having a health problem or issue. You may have a problem with your back that prevents you from doing certain things. This is understandable – however, if that is then being used as an excuse for not doing other things you are really just scared of doing – a lack of confidence is really your underlying reason.

What Are The End Results?

A person with low self confidence will be left feeling:

- frustrated
- disappointed
- frightened and vulnerable
- fearful
- stressed and tense

They will also become stagnant and stuck, as they are too fearful to move forward with their life. This in turn, will have a negative effect on their self esteem – which is why they so often go hand-in-hand.

What Causes Low Self Confidence and How Can I Solve It?

We have covered the symptoms of low self esteem and low confidence, so how do we actually solve these problems? This is covered in depth within the chapters of Section 2. For the time being, we will look at the remaining 8 commonly asked questions.

*"You may feel like dwelling on your limits or your fears.
Don't do it. A perfect prescription
for a squandered, unfulfilled life is to accommodate self-defeating feelings while
undercutting your finest, most productive ones."*

– Marsha Sinetar

QUESTION 3

"Every achiever that I have ever met says, 'My life turned around when I began to believe in me,'"

– Dr. Robert H Schuller

What Causes Low Self Confidence & Low Self Esteem?

Before we look at making steps to solving our low confidence and esteem, we need to know what causes us personally to have these issues as, unless you find the root cause of your low confidence and esteem, any efforts you make to solve it will only be short term and temporary – like sticking a plaster over them.

You need to get to the root cause and solve that problem to give your confidence and esteem room to grow. I will be helping you with discovering the root causes of your low confidence and self esteem in the subsequent sections of this book. For the purposes of this chapter however, I have given an overview of the common causes of low confidence and esteem.

Your Environment

Your immediate environment may play a part in you having high or low confidence and esteem. When you look around the rooms in your home and/or work, they will either inspire or deflate you. Do you live in such a sterile environment that you feel restricted by rules and regulations; do you feel free to express yourself, make a mess, lose control?

Equally, do you live in such an untidy environment that you feel so burdened down with the enormity of the mess around you? Do you crave a section of uncluttered space to give you a feeling of space and freshness?

Maybe your environment is too noisy or quiet? Depending on the type of person you are, the noise or quiet will either inspire you or deflate you. Maybe noise helps you feel energised and alive; maybe you need quiet to hear your thoughts, to be calm.

The People Around You

The people you surround you with are quite important to your confidence and esteem too. Your friends and family may be unsupportive of you, instilling and confirming the negative viewpoint you have of yourself.

Sometimes, the people around you will make you feel too safe and secure. If you are scared to try something new, these well-meaning relatives and friends will point out that you are better off staying put, as it's a big, bad world out there. They will sense your fear and, in an effort to protect you from potential upset or disappointment, will point out all the benefits of what you currently have.

The problem with surrounding yourself with likeminded people is that misery attracts misery. You all gain a comfort from being around similar people, so if one of you wants to change, the others will want to resist you changing, as it will have an effect on them and their feelings of security.

Your Inner Thought Patterns

As already touched upon, the thoughts that run around in your mind will have a large impact on your confidence and esteem. Someone may have made a passing comment about your appearance or your inability to do something that tweaked a negative emotion in you. Your brain then linked that emotion with that statement, making that comment more important to remember – after all, we don't like the feeling of any negative emotion.

The problem is, that statement is then stored with that emotion attached. Next time you feel that emotion, or someone says something about your abilities or appearance, your brain links it with that negative emotion again. Before long, you have a pattern developing that says 'people comment about my abilities/appearance: I feel bad. I feel bad because I cannot do xyz/my appearance is 'abnormal' in some way: I feel bad.. It will then look for data to confirm or dispel their comments. Data with an emotion attached will be at the front of the queue – so any strong negative (or positive) data will be there.

We continually look for data to reinforce our negative or positive opinions. If you have a negative opinion of your appearance, your brain will focus on things to back this up and it will filter out any positive things as irrelevant or unimportant. Whether you think or say a negative comment about your appearance – it will store this as relevant. If someone else says something negative about your appearance – it will store this with the other relevant pieces of information, thus reinforcing your negative opinion.

Your Belief Structure

Your beliefs are made up of sweeping statements, backed up with relevant data. You have been building beliefs since you were a child, so your upbringing will have played a part in your beliefs.

If your mother stayed at home whilst your father worked, and you were frequently told 'wait until your father gets home' when you had been naughty, then you will have deduced several possible beliefs from this:

- mums (females) stay home

- dads (males) bring in the money
- dads (males) are the authority
- dads (males) are the disciplinarians
- mums (females) are the peace keepers
- mums (females) are meek and mild
- dads (males) are strong and tough
- dads (males) word is law
- mums (females) lower than dad (males)

Your Upbringing

As touched on above, your upbringing will have a large impact on your confidence and esteem, as it will have effected your environment, included the people around you (many of which are probably still around you), been the main force in building your belief structure and all of which would have had a knock-on effect on your inner thought patterns.

Our Beliefs About Love

I believe that feeling unworthy of love is one of the biggest reasons for low self esteem in women, often because we are ruled by our emotions. When we are little, our parents are our role models, not only playing a part in building our belief structure, but emotionally too. If we felt that their love was conditional and dependant on how we behaved, we'd do our best to make sure that we behaved well. I believe this is where we start learning to please everyone else.

We are bought up on romantic fairy tales of rather needy, sometimes pathetically weak princesses finding love with a handsome prince who comes to their rescue – this reinforces the fact that females are weak and males are strong.

As we get older, we spend our younger years – sometimes, even our whole life – looking for our 'other half' that elusive other person who has the magical ability to make us feel 'whole' and totally adored and loved. We then marry, often giving up our own surname to take on another 'identity'; we are now a wife.

We then play this role, a lot of the time believing our husbands are the 'one in charge' before we have children and take on another new role – the role of 'mother'. We then cater for the needs of our children; putting both our husband and our children's needs before our own – as this is what we have been bought up to do – and it's all because we love them.

This is all great if it is done for the right reasons – I know, I am a mother and wife myself, and the joy of raising a child and being with a man who loves and respects you is inspiring – however, sometimes women go into relationships driven by a need to be whole/complete and loved; a need to prove they are lovable and worthy of being loved. Sometimes we have the mentality that we may not love (or even like) ourselves, but if we find someone who does like/love us, then we might either change our opinion of ourselves or at least be happy.

We don't always compute the fact we are complete and whole as an individual – and that the greatest gift you can give yourself is to actually love yourself as a person.

Summary

We've covered what low self confidence and low self esteem are, along with what symptoms and characteristics a person suffering from them may have. We have just covered the areas that may cause low confidence and esteem, so now we will be looking at the remaining six commonly asked questions related to self confidence and self esteem, in the following chapters.

"A man travels the world over in search of what he needs and returns home to find it."

– George Moore

QUESTION 4

"It has been said that our anxiety does not empty tomorrow of its sorrow, but only empties today of its strength."

– Charles Haddon Spurgeon

What is Anxiety and How Do You Overcome It?

Anxiety is a behavioural condition that causes a feeling, similar to fear. Unlike fear however, you often don't know what you are actually anxious about. It is perfectly natural to feel some anxiety at different stages of your life – however it only becomes a problem if it affects your daily life; especially if the danger has long passed – or in the absence of any real threat in the first place.

Anxiety not only affects how you feel, it also affects how you behave – and has some very real physical symptoms. It can also lead to panic attacks (a state of irrational fear that comes on without warning) that may result in you feeling as if you are about to lose consciousness.

What Are The Symptoms of Anxiety?

Think how you feel when you are nervous. These are the typical symptoms of anxiety. Apart from a general overall feeling of apprehension and worry, some of the more physical symptoms include:

- trembling
- feeling tearful and irritable
- pounding heartbeat
- chest pains
- churning stomach
- muscle tension
- feeling sick and/or faint
- headache
- tiredness/difficulty sleeping
- sweating

Some people have more severe physical symptoms such as heart palpitations and numbness in the hands, arms and legs and, if your anxiety is long-term, it may cause hypertension (high blood pressure). It's then easy to become even more anxious as you fear you are suffering from something much worse – such as a heart attack or stroke.

How Does Anxiety Affect You?

Suffering from anxiety will affect your life in different ways including:

- reduced ability to cope with day-to-day life
- difficulty in holding down a job or relationship
- withdrawing from having contact with other people (including friends and family)
- obsessive thoughts and repeated behaviour patterns (such as endlessly washing your hands)

What Causes Anxiety?

Anxiety can be caused by several things. I have listed the most common causes, as:

Stress
Stress is one of the common triggers for anxiety. The habit of using negative self talk and constantly focusing on the worst outcome will also make anxiety rear its head.

Worrying about the future
Anxiety can also be caused by you worrying about the future. It is easy to feel as if we have no control of the different aspects of our lives. Potential events, such as being attacked, developing an illness or disease and even the fear of nuclear war can all be the root cause of our stress.

Early role models
The anxiety we feel can also be a response learned from early in our life. If the members of your family always see the world as a fearful place, you will have picked up on this and carried it into your adult life.

Diet and lifestyle
What we eat and drink (such as excessive caffeine, sugar and a poor diet in general) can cause us to suffer from anxiety, as well as drug misuse and side effects of certain medication.

How Do You Solve An Anxiety Problem?

Steering clear of situations that make you anxious will help you in the short term; however the relief is only temporary. You will also be more inclined to avoid more and more situations – and find it harder to face that situation if it should arise in future.

So, what is the best way of dealing with anxiety?

- One of the top causes of anxiety is stress, so it makes sense to learn to manage those stressful situations and events in your life.
- Work on your negative self talk. You've already seen how this can affect your confidence and esteem, so this highlights just another area it can affect.
- Look into relaxation techniques such as yoga and meditation
- Learning how to be assertive
- Learning self-defence (to make you feel safer in general)
- Limit your caffeine, alcohol and nicotine intake
- Exercise – to use up the hormones that stress produces, as well as relaxing muscles and allowing you to sleep better.
- Talk the problem through with a friend or member of your family

Speak To Your GP

If your anxiety is severe and/or you are suffering from some of the more extreme symptoms, it is worth visiting your local GP. If you are in any doubt, I would always suggest you seek medical advice, as there are certain medications and therapies that they may be able to prescribe and recommend, to enable you to get your anxiety down to more normal levels.

"We can't fear the past. Fear is a future thing. And since the future's all in
our heads, fear must be a head thing."

– Tom Payne

QUESTION 5

*"If you want to be happy, set a goal that commands your thoughts,
liberates your energy, and inspires your hopes."*

– Andrew Carnegie

Why Do I Feel So Low?

There could be many reasons for feeling generally low. Everyone experiences emotional ups and downs at various times in their lives, depending on what is going on, however If there are no obvious causes for your feeling low, then the cause may be a related to your confidence and/or esteem.

Breaking those low feelings down to core basics, and all the different reasons tend to have a common root cause – one (or more) of the areas in your life needs putting back on track.

I am not trying to be to blasé about it, as it can have symptoms that can drastically affect your daily life, but that is the bottom line. The difficulty tends to be finding which area needs sorting. This general low feeling, if left to continue for any length of time, runs the risk of turning into full-blown depression.

What Symptoms Are There?

As mentioned above, symptoms can really affect your daily life. Symptoms to watch for can include:

- Feeling restless and agitated
- Feeling tired and lacking energy
- Not wanting to talk or interact with other people
- Drastic changes in your eating, drinking and sleeping patterns
- Generally finding everyday things too hard to cope with
- Feeling more emotional/being more tearful
- Using drugs or alcohol as a way of coping
- Not taking care of yourself (including feeling as if you don't matter)

How Will Feeing So Low Affect You?

Feeling low will affect your daily life in different ways, similar to all the previous chapters. As it will affect you in various areas of your life, the end results will include:

- reduced ability to cope with day-to-day life
- difficulty in holding down a job or relationship
- withdrawing from having contact with other people (including friends and family)
- obsessive thoughts and repeated behaviour patterns (such as endlessly washing your hands)
- feeling frightened and vulnerable
- stressed and tense
- stagnant, no energy, spirit is trapped – no sense of connection
- closed to new possibilities
- weak personal power
- no defence against challenges life may throw your way
- feeling like you have nowhere to turn

What Causes Me To Feel So Low?

Obviously, this will vary depending on your individual circumstances, however some of the more common reasons (related to self confidence and self esteem) may include:

- lack of motivation
- unhappy with environment around you
- unhappy with yourself
- your own inner self talk

We will be creating a targeted action plan for you in Sections 2 and 3, however for the purposes of this question, let's take a look at these areas in a bit more detail.

Lack of Motivation

Do you know what direction you want to take in the different areas of your life? Sometimes we lack motivation purely because we don't actually know where we're headed! Maybe you know what you want to do, but have no clear plans or goals – leaving you to feel like an unanchored boat drifting along with the tides.

Just thinking about your goals and ambitions should make you feel excited. If they leave you feeling deflated and flat – maybe you should look at changing them slightly or examining your real reasons for wanting to achieve them.

Unhappy With Your Environment

This could include your home environment, work-related space and also the people around you. Does your home environment make you feel depressed and low? If you could make any changes, what would they be?

It's the same with the people you hang out with. Is there a particular person whose presence makes you feel lower the moment they enter the room?

Unhappy With Yourself

As we've seen in the previous chapters, how you see your self image and what you think generally about you, can have quite an impact on your life. Your upbringing, unresolved issues, belief structure and your own inner talk can all play a part in your unhappiness.

Being unhappy with yourself in general, along with a general feeling of lowness are all signs that you are not connected to self.

This is such an in depth broad subject, that I cannot hope to cover it all in this chapter, let alone this Book, which is why this is just a first step in your journey of better confidence and esteem.

Building your motivation and addressing the different areas of your life will be explained and detailed in other courses, directly related to those subjects.

Inner Self Talk

This has been discussed in previous chapters, however it is worth remembering that the way you talk and think about yourself and the environment around will have a noticeable impact on your personality and your emotional well being.

How Do I Solve This Problem?

Get a Plan in Place

Use Section 2 of this book to work on a clear action plan for yourself. This will enable you to have some clear, focused action steps to take, moving your focus onto better things as well as keeping you motivated.

Work On Your Self Confidence and/or Esteem

Use this Book as a starting point to work on your confidence and esteem, to build them up to healthier, more positive levels. You can also enrol on a course dedicated to building self confidence and esteem, to work on them in greater detail.

Talk To Someone

Sometimes the very act of talking to someone about how low you feel can play a part in changing it for the better. Find a sympathetic friend, family member or even your GP, will all be a suitable match.

Focus On The Positive

It is so easy to talk about and focus on the negative situations in our life. However in doing so, we are not actually helping ourselves – we are just keeping those negative thoughts and feelings at the front of our consciousness.

I am not asking you to pretend those negative things don't exist, but I am asking you to spend time looking for positive people and situations to focus on instead. The very act of being grateful for those positive things will enable your mind to actively seek out more of those things to make you feel happier.

Get checked out by your GP

It is worth going and getting checked out by your GP, as the symptoms listed above can also appear for other medical conditions including:

- Underactive thyroid
- Depression
- Seasonal Affected Disorder (SAD)

If in any doubt, seek the advice of your GP, as all the conditions above can be easily diagnosed and treated.

*"Happiness is to be found along the way, not at the end of the road, for then
the journey is over and it is too late.
Today, this hour, this minute is the day, the hour, the minute for each of us to
sense the fact that life is good, with all of its trials and troubles,
and perhaps more interesting because of them."*

– Robert R Updegraff

QUESTION 6

*"Until you are happy with who you are,
you will never be happy because of what you have."*

– Zig Ziglar

Why Am I Unhappy?

This question frequently ties in with the previous question: 'Why Do I Feel So Low?' Feeling unhappy is our body's way of highlighting to us that something 'isn't right'. Your body and your emotions are the best built-in guidance system you have. This is why a lot of the best descriptive sayings we use involve how we feel. For example: 'I have a gut feeling', 'it just doesn't feel right' and 'I can feel it in my bones.'

The unhappiness you are feeling will, most often, affect one or two areas of your life. If it is effecting all the areas of your life you will need to ascertain which area(s) are the root cause, as the chances are it's had a knock-on effect on those other areas. (how to do this will be explained later in this book).

What symptoms Are There?

Symptoms are very similar to those listed in the previous chapter. As a reminder, the symptoms to watch out for include:

- Feeling restless and agitated
- Feeling tired and lacking energy
- Not wanting to talk or interact with other people

- Drastic changes in your eating, drinking and sleeping patterns
- Generally finding everyday things too hard to cope with
- Feeling more emotional/being more tearful
- Using drugs or alcohol as a way of coping
- Not taking care of yourself (including feeling as if you don't matter)
- A few other symptoms that are quite common with general unhappiness include:
- Feeling as if your emotions have 'flat-lined'
- Feeling that everything is just too much effort

A general feeling of heaviness (as if you have your own personal raincloud following you around)

It's very easy, when you are feeling unhappy, to give yourself a hard time. Other people don't always understand either and will come out with comments like: 'Why don't you just get a grip?' or 'Cheer up, it can't be that bad.' You may even be using these comments to beat yourself up, but if you do not solve the root problem of your unhappiness and actually deal with it you will run the risk of it manifesting as full blown depression.

How Will Feeing So Unhappy Affect You?

Feeling low and feeling unhappy are very similar, and so will affect your daily life in the same way. To recap, these end results will include:

- reduced ability to cope with day-to-day life
- difficulty in holding down a job or relationship
- withdrawing from having contact with other people (including friends and family)

- obsessive thoughts and repeated behaviour patterns (such as endlessly washing your hands)
- feeling frightened and vulnerable
- stressed and tense
- stagnant, no energy spirit is trapped – no sense of connection
- closed to new possibilities
- weak personal power
- no defence against challenges life may throw your way
- feeling like you have nowhere to turn

What Causes Me To Feel So Unhappy?

As already mentioned in the previous chapter, common reasons for feeling low and/or unhappy include:

- lack of motivation
- unhappy with home environment
- unhappy with self
- Inner self talk

However, there are also other reasons for being unhappy and these include:

- knowing something is wrong
- feeling need for change
- don't know where to start
- not living to your belief structure

These four reasons are really a step forward! I know that may be hard to believe at the moment, so let me explain.

Quite often, these four reasons that follow are making you unhappy <u>because you know there is a problem.</u> Nine times out of ten <u>you also know what that problem is</u>. So, you are a step closer to solving your unhappiness!

Now we will cover these in greater detail.

Knowing Something Is Wrong

When you know something is wrong in your current lifestyle or personality, you are faced with two scenarios:

- knowing something is wrong but you're unsure as to what it is
- knowing something is wrong and you know what it is

The fact you have listened to your body and the messages it has been sending out, needs to be acknowledged. Why? Because not everyone will know something is wrong. They will feel unhappy, but will not know that anything directly involving them is the issue! They spend their time looking outside and blaming others for their unhappiness.

So, allow yourself a few minutes to mentally pat yourself on the back for noticing you have something that needs sorting!

If you're already sure of what that something is – great! If you're unsure what it is – we will cover this later in this chapter.

Feeling A Need For Change

This is similar to knowing something is wrong, but the signals you are receiving are coming more from an emotional level.

Again, give yourself a few minutes to pat yourself on the back for listening to those emotions – as not everyone will take notice of them and they are trying to draw your attention to an issue.

Overwhelm

If you are unhappy because you don't know where to start, this is usually down to two reasons: a) there are too many areas affected, or b) the problem feels too big to solve. Either way, you are being overwhelmed. The problem with overwhelm is that you can end up feeling stuck and too scared to move towards a solution – and this will lead to more unhappiness.

Not Living To Your Belief Structure

Your belief structure is the core set of beliefs that you live your daily life by. These beliefs are what govern how you think, talk and act. They are made up of <u>how and what you think and believe</u>, along with <u>why you think and believe what you do</u>, about the world and yourself.

We look for evidence to back up our belief structure, as we go about our daily lives. So for example, if you have 'you must be honest' as one of your beliefs, and your job involves you telling little white lies to you customers – you will be going against one of your core beliefs – and if this is continued over a long period of time – your happiness will be affected.

Focusing On The Negative/Filtering Out The Positive

There is a saying that the British love moaning. We will moan about everything from the weather to the queue in the supermarket. In reality, moaning about the various things that annoy us isn't limited to just the Brits – we all love a good moan.

The problem is that when we moan about something, our focus is on the thing we are moaning about – and quite often leads us to thinking it is worse than it is. This isn't too bad if you are talking about a queue you are standing in, but when we are talking about events in our life – it is easy to make them seem worse than they are.

This leads us to focus more on these issues – not only making them seem bigger again, but it also gives rise to another problem.

By focusing on the negative, we can often filter out anything positive that may happen. To use a simple example: you may have got out of bed late, dressed in a hurry and now think you look a mess and your day is going to be rubbish. You become so focused on having a rubbish day that when a rather attractive man smiles at you, your first thought is 'OMG, he's smiling because I look a mess!' So, you put your head down, blush and remind yourself that your day has just gotten worse. The positive possibilities relating to him smiling at you (including the fact he found you attractive and has possibility been building up to making the first move for weeks!) do not even enter your mind.

How Do I Solve This Problem of Unhappiness?

If you know what your problem is, you can skip the first step and start with brainstorming. If you don't know what the problem is or the area in your life your unhappiness is stemming from, you will need to start with:

Assessing Your Current Situation

The first thing you will need to do is assess your current situation. Look at all areas of your life, including your finances, relationships, career, and you personally. The aim of this is to find out what areas are causing your unhappiness. You can then break down the area(s) of concern and narrow it down to the root problems that are making you unhappy.

Brainstorm

Now you know what the root problems are, you need to brainstorm all possible solutions – no matter how big or small they are. You are looking at what would be your 'ideal world' solution to both this area of your life and the problem at hand.

Take your time covering all the areas affected and don't limit yourself due to any restraints (such as finances, peer pressure, qualifications etc).

Now, narrow your solutions down to those that 'feel' right, those that make you feel happier and calmer – listen to your gut!

Break Down Into Manageable Chunks

You can now figure out the steps needed, to take you from where you are to where you want to be. Depending on how much work is involved and how big a change the solution is you will have a varying amount of steps. Don't worry about how many steps you have to take to get to your end result – focus on the fact you are moving towards it.

Figure What Your First Step Will Be

Now figure out what your first step will be. If your goal is to move areas, your first step may involve finding out about, or evening visiting, other areas you may want to live in. If you goal is to have a change of career, your first step may involve either looking at enrolling for new qualifications or looking in the local paper for job vacancies.

Take Action!

You final step is to complete that first step! Focus only on the individual step you are on at that moment in time, as focusing on the end result may cause you to feel overwhelmed with the remaining steps. Just remember to remind yourself that you are taking steps to improve your situation.

Quite often the process of actually facing the areas that are causing your unhappiness, along with having an action plan of steps in place, is enough to start easing your unhappiness.

Get checked out by your GP

As mentioned in the previous chapter, it is worth going and getting checked out by your GP, as the symptoms listed above can also appear for other medical conditions including:

- Underactive thyroid
- Depression
- Seasonal Affected Disorder (SAD)

If in any doubt, seek the advice of your GP, as all the conditions above can be easily diagnosed and treated.

> *"Most people are about as happy as they make up their minds to be."*
>
> – Ben Franklin

QUESTION 7

"Always be a first-rate version of yourself, instead of a second-rate version of someone else."

– Judy Garland

Why Am I Ugly?

Did you know that Google Adwords shows that the estimated traffic from people searching this question is approximately 61,000 people each month!!

It is amazing that so many people have this question on their mind; enough to actually search for an answer on the internet. It highlights that so many people believe they have this issue – when in reality, the problem isn't how they look – it's how they THINK they look; to themselves and others. It is a **negative belief** they hold about themselves.

Another point worth remembering is that appearance isn't the only measure of ugliness. Your character and personality also play a part in how attractive you are. We all know someone who we consider as 'average' looking, who seems to glow like a lighthouse, attracting all the people to them – people who enjoy this persons company and who cannot speak highly enough about them.

As a human being, you are unique. We all share common elements but we are all unique in different ways; our appearance, personality and character. We may have had the same upbringing or big life events as the person next to us, but how we dealt with and analysed those events will have caused us to be different in our outlook and character as a result.

You see, the way you view your appearance is actually a result of having a low self image (Which stems from having a low self esteem). As we have covered dealing with low self esteem in the previous chapters, I will both recap and add a few extra pertinent comments below.

Now, you may want to argue with me right about now. You may be hollering even: 'that's alright for you Sarah, but I AM UGLY!' I'm here to tell you that this is just a belief you hold – you are not ugly! Now give me a chance and read the rest of this chapter!

The Symptoms & End Results of Holding This Belief

You may believe that there are no symptoms – apart from thinking you are ugly. And that is just a thought right? The beliefs you hold about your appearance can affect your day-to-day lives, as well as your career. A person who thinks they are unattractive will often cut themselves off from meeting new people as well as limiting contact with close family and friends.

The truth is, holding the belief that you are ugly will potentially affect every area of your life.

Sometimes you will hold a belief that you don't deserve to have a relationship – and if you are in a relationship, the person is only with you out of pity or duty – so it can have a negative effect on your relationships.

Your sense of self worth is affected, so your career and finance areas will suffer. As a result of your low self worth, you won't be bothered to spend too much time (if any) on your appearance. You may even go in the opposite direction and spend hours on your appearance but are still not be happy with the end result.

Due to the long term negative thoughts that you are analysing over and over again, your actual health will eventually suffer – from general unhappiness right through to full blown depression, and the symptoms that brings.

So, believing you are ugly isn't just a thought about your looks – it can have a major physical effect on your entire life.

What Causes Me To Hold This Belief About Myself?

There are four core main reasons that may have caused you to hold this belief:

- your upbringing
- The people around you
- other people's viewpoints
- you inner self talk

We have covered all of them in the previous chapters of this Book, but **I cannot stress enough how much influence we give to these four areas.**

Your opinions about your looks will likely stem from one of these areas. You may have had the original thought, but it is often how others react to this opinion that will help dispel it – or cement it deeper inside your mind.

That old chestnut of a saying: 'sticks and stones may break my bones, but words will never hurt me', really should carry a warning at the end of it. Words may not physically hurt you – but the damage they can do mentally, really can take years to heal. And this isn't limited to what others say to us – we can do just as much damage to ourselves with our own inner self talk!

How Do I Solve The Problem of Having This Belief?

As stated earlier in this chapter, the best way of solving this negative belief is to work on your self esteem. We will be looking at beliefs in more detail in Sections 2 and 3. In the meantime, you can also improve how you see your own self image and appearance by following this mini action plan.

Action Plan for Your Appearance

Assess your current situation.

Look at yourself in a mirror and make a list of positives you see. This can be anything related to your facial features, figure, hair, stature, dress sense etc – and remember to assess your character and attitude too! I want you to stay looking at that mirror until you have at least 3 things written down. If you are really struggling, rephrase the question to 'what do I consider to be passable about me?' or 'what is least irritating or annoying about me?' Maybe you like the colour of your eyes, or your hair styles really easily, or you like the freckles over your nose – whatever it is write it down.

Focus on those positives.

Sit and make a list of any positive comments people have previously said to you. From today onwards I want you to add any new positive comments and compliments you are given – no matter how small they may seem. If someone says your hair looks good today, or they like your outfit, write it down.

Enhance those positives.

Using the previous two steps as a guide, make a point of enhancing those good bits. If you decided you liked your eyes, enhance them by wearing makeup or having your eyebrows plucked. If you liked your nails, paint them. Maybe you liked your cleavage or narrow waist – so wear a top that shows it off to its full advantage. If one of your good points was your approachability, make a point of approaching more people and making that first move in conversation.

Reinforce those positives.
Take time to look in the mirror (daily!) and compliment yourself on those parts of you that you find positive. Actually state it out loud!

Praise where praise is due.
Paying a compliment to someone else about their appearance will not only make their day, but yours too – and you may even end up making more friends! Take the time to notice other people's good points – in both their appearance and their personality. Pay compliments that are deserved and remind yourself that you are making their day.

Work on your negatives.
Those parts you consider to be negative can be improved – and if you cannot improve them you can change your attitude towards them. Let's say for example, you dislike the fact you are short. You can dress to give the illusion of height, you can change the focus to your personality, or you can accept you are short and embrace it totally – as is often quoted: the best things come in small packages!

Remember you are unique.
We are all unique. We have our own quirks, personalities and characters. What one person sees as attractive and positive – another may see as unattractive and negative. After all, if we all found the same people attractive we'd all be queuing to be the next Mrs Brad Pitt rather than the next Mrs Bill Gates! (See, this is my own personal opinion as opposed to true fact!)

Even the most attractive people will have off days. You only have to look at all those celebrities and film stars that are photographed on the red carpet, at posh hotels and on holiday. They all look amazing after spending hours with the hairdresser and make-up artists. Then look at the candid snaps of them taken without their knowledge; emptying their dustbins, the day after the movie premier and suffering from a hangover...

*"A lot of disappointed people have been left standing on the
street corner waiting for the bus marked Perfection."*

– Donald Kennedy

QUESTION 8

*"Once you take action there is no such thing as failure.
There are only experiences, decisions and their
consequences, and results.
The only real failure is not having a go in the first place."*

– Fiona Harrold

Why Do I Feel Like A Failure?

It is amazing that so many people have this question on their mind. It highlights how much emphasis we put on succeeding – whether that be in our general day-to-day life (such as relationships and finances) or in our career and work life.

This question is similar to the previous one – it is a **negative belief** we may be holding about ourselves. We will be creating an action plan to deal with your low self confidence and self esteem, as well as going into more details with beliefs you hold in Sections 2 and 3, however for the purposes of answering this question, I have given a brief overview in this chapter.

Your view on success and failure is often linked to your levels of confidence and self esteem. As we have covered dealing with low self confidence and self esteem in the previous chapters, I will add a few pertinent comments, directly related to this negative belief below.

What Symptoms Are There For This Belief?

It's easy to say that the symptoms for feeling like a failure are just that – you feel like a failure. However, this belief you are holding will have other, seemingly unrelated symptoms. These include:

- changes in your eating and drinking routines
- changes in your sleeping patterns – either sleeping lots or not enough
- depression
- tiredness and/or lethargy
- lack of motivation
- feeling generally sick or unwell

As this is a belief, rather than a physical ailment, the symptoms you show can affect your physical and mental health in a variety of ways, so this belief can affect different parts of your life too.

What Causes Me To Feel This Way?

Feeling like a failure can have several root causes. I will cover the more common reasons below.

How we measure success and failure

One of the more common reasons for feeling like a failure can be put down to how we actually measure success and failure. Sometimes we don't even have a rule to measure against! It can be awfully difficult to judge whether you have succeeded at something, if you don't know what the end result will look like.

Sometimes we can make success dependent on such a stringent set of tiny criteria, we will feel as if we have failed if we are unable to tick the boxes for all of those criteria. For example, your measure of success when achieving your dream job is:

- earning £55,000 per annum
- being a size 8
- married by the time you are 30 years old
- working 9-5.30 Monday to Wednesday
- manager of a department with 30 employees
- wearing suits tailor made for me
- wearing Jimmy Choo shoes
- driving a Jaguar convertible

If you end up earning £25,000 BUT have to work Monday to Friday to achieve that income and you're only driving a Mercedes – does that mean you failed? For the people who have set that success bar so specific, the answer will be yes, meaning they will actually feel like they've failed. So you've achieved 99.9% of what you set out to achieve; the fact that you didn't achieve that last 0.1% - do you still consider it a failure or success?

Who's Viewpoint we are using

Let's continue with the dream job example above and this time you have actually achieved all those criteria – but you're still not happy as you still don't feel like you've succeeded. What could be the problem now?

The problem may well be you are using someone else's viewpoint or measure as your success and failure rule. Maybe that dream job is actually your father or mother's idea of success and not yours. Alternatively, you could be happy with that dream job, but you don't feel like you've succeeded as your parents, friends or neighbours have belittled your achievement. This then runs on to the next reason:

Focusing on the negatives

We could have achieved all of what we set out to achieve, but we still haven't got the respect of our peers, family and friends or our neighbours. Some would view this negative as a measure of failure.

It could be that you achieved 75% of what you set out to achieve, but you consider it a failure as you are focusing on the 25% you didn't achieve.

If your focus is on the negative results of what you've achieved, you will consider the achievement as a failure.

Sabotaging your success

The last common reason for feeling like a failure is actually a fear of success. You may, or not be consciously sabotaging your success efforts, but you're sabotaging them if you are guilty of any of the following:

- not putting 100% of your efforts into achieving the end result
- procrastinating in your efforts
- talking about the end results but not actually doing anything towards them
- putting off starting them until you have time, the right tools, the right day, you feel less tired ... (you can put any excuse in here!)
- you're thinking about what other people will think of the end result of your efforts

All of these are common ways of sabotaging your success – and they are all a result of a fear of success. It could be that you are scared to start, because you feel safe in your current comfort zone; or maybe you are worried how other people will treat you differently, once you have reached your goal, but this all falls under the category of being scared of success. This will then lead you to either sabotage your efforts – or not even start at all.

How Do I Solve The Problem of This Negative Belief?

As with all negative beliefs, there are a few simple things you can do to take steps forward. An overview of these steps includes:

Get in the right frame of mind

Make sure you are measuring your success by your own rule, rather than someone else's. Are the things you want to achieve actually what **you** want? Spend time deciding how you will measure your success – don't make it to rigid, allow some room for adapting.

Focus on the positives

When you achieve anything, make sure you spend some time acknowledging the positives of that achievement – no matter how big or small. Reward yourself for those positives.

Change your limiting belief

Your limiting belief is currently 'I feel like a failure'; now decide to change it to 'I feel like a success'. Look for evidence to back up this new belief by examining all your past achievements.

Stop comparing yourself to others

By focusing on what other people have, you are not actually seeing what you have. Wean yourself off comparing yourself to others by moving your focus onto what you have. The problem with using comparison as a success gauge is you will always find something (or someone) who will have something bigger, better, shinier than you.

Learn to be grateful for what you have, along with what you achieve.

"You may have a fresh start any moment you choose, for this thing we call failure is not the falling down, but the staying down."

– Mary Pickford

QUESTION 9

"One of the most tragic things I know about human nature is that all of us tend to put off living. We are all dreaming of some magical rose garden over the horizon – instead of enjoying the roses blooming outside our windows today."

– Dale Carnegie

What Do I Really Want?

This is one of those questions so frequently asked – but seldom answered. Some people spend their whole life puzzling over this, with no satisfying conclusion in sight. They look for external references, read all the latest books relating to living your ideal life and seek other people's opinions to help guide them towards their own answers.

I personally think we all want two things – love and happiness – but these come in different guises for everyone. Some women want independence and no relationships, others want a relationship and commitments; some want a career, others want to me a mother to a huge family. But even these answers can be brainstormed into further niches – what type of family, what type of career, where to live, who to live with etc.

Only you can answer this question

Therefore, this question really isn't something anyone else can give you the answer to. You are the only person who can answer this question – as you will have your own ideas and plans; those things you want to have and do. Giving yourself time to really think about what you want out of life – and allowing yourself to dream big when thinking about this question – is all you really need to do to find your own answer.

Each individual is unique, and as a result, different areas affect them in different ways. What I can do however, is give you a few stepping stones in the right direction to assist you in finding your own answer to this question.

So what are those areas? Some of the more common areas are summarised below.

Your beliefs

As previously touched on, the beliefs you hold are what you use to live your life by. Each individual will have their own set, based on evidence they have accumulated during their life. One person may believe it is wrong to lie, another may believe it is alright in certain situations. Knowing what those strong beliefs are will help you get clear on what will make you happy.

Environment

Your surrounding environment plays a part in working out what you want. This includes the people around you. If you are living in a poorer part of the world then your answer to 'what do I really want?' will be totally different to anyone living in one of the more affluent countries.

The people around you will also play a part in your answer, as you may want to include (or exclude) them in your answer.

Upbringing

Whether you were bought up as a religious person, your gender and your age will all have an impact on your reply to this question. Your parents, for example, may be your role model for what you want, or even what you don't want.

What makes you happy?

Getting clear on what makes you happy is a good stepping stone to knowing what you want out of life. Could what makes you happy be used more in your life? Could it become part of a career or lifestyle? As a general rule of thumb, finding out what makes you happy, and then doing more of it, is always a good starting point!

How Can I Improve My Chances?

You can summarise it using the following steps:

- give yourself time to really think about this questions
- get clear on what you currently have
- get clear on who you want to be
- get clear on what you want to achieve
- describe your ideal day, week, year etc
- do more of what makes you happy

We cover this all in greater detail in Sections 2 and 3, however the bottom line is once you have looked at the points above – move on with your life. Life the life you currently have to its fullest capacity, **whilst** looking for your answer to this question – don't delay on living your life **until** you have the answer – otherwise you will look back at a life full of regret.

"Live with intention. Walk to the edge. Listen hard. Practice wellness. Play with abandon. Laugh. Choose with no regret. Continue to learn. Appreciate your friends. Do what you love. Live as if this is all there is."

– Mary Ann Roadacher-Hershey

QUESTION 10

*"Think positively and masterfully, with confidence and faith,
and life becomes more secure, more fraught with action, richer in achievement and experience."*

– Eddie Rickenbacker

How Do You Stay Positive?

The topic of motivation and positivity is large enough to have a book all to itself however I will try to give you enough information to get you started. Staying positive can be quite difficult when you are faced with challenging situations – and even challenging people. So to answer this question you first need to get more specific.

What areas are you looking at?

You need to know what areas of your life you are struggling to stay motivated with, before you can actually work on staying positive. So narrow it down, for example are you looking to boost your positivity in:

- your lifestyle
- your work/career
- personally (confidence, esteem, happiness etc)
- with goal setting

Obviously goal setting is another topic all to itself, but all the above areas will have things in common. The fact that you need help staying positive is a signal that something is not quite right. Below I have listed some common reasons that encompass all the areas mentioned.

Possible Causes For Struggling With Positivity

In order to be positive about something you need to be able to see a positive, happy outcome at the end. Whether you are working on goals related to your personal life, career or personal development, you need to have an overwhelming reason to reach your end target. So, with that in mind, let's look at the possible causes for struggling to stay positive.

No goal or plan

If you read the paragraph above and thought to yourself: 'Plan? What plan?' then this is the most obvious reason for you struggling to stay positive. We need to know we are headed to a better end result. We also need to know we are working for a reason. Whether that reason is financial or personal, you need to get clear on why you are doing something – and for what reason.

Another part of this is planning. As the well-known saying goes – 'If you fail to plan, you plan to fail'. As with any goal setting, if you know the start and end places, you can compile a set of steps to get from one to the other.

Wrong goal

Look at the reason why you want to achieve what you want to are aiming for. If you are going into it for the wrong reasons or it may cause distress or upset to people you care about, then maybe that goal isn't right for you.

Whilst looking at your reasons you may realise you're actually doing it either for other people or because of other people. You will struggle to stay motivated and positive if you are heading for an end result you don't even want.

Not enough stimulation

Another reason you may be struggling to stay positive is you aren't motivated enough to stay positive. If this is the case, then you need to remind yourself what you will gain and achieve from whatever you are doing. Imagine the end result, whether it's a new job or a new you, picture it in glorious Technicolor, use all your senses and make it look big, bright and colourful.

Focusing on the negative

As mentioned in earlier chapters, having your focus on the wrong thing will not help you stay positive. If you are focusing on the negativity around you, it will drag you down – whether that is people or situations and places. Switch your focus to the positives – your outcome, friends and family, compliments, nice weather etc – anything to switch your focus to the positives.

Steps To Help You Stay Positive

Switching the causes around will give you the steps you need to help you stay positive.

- get a goal and plan in place
- make sure you are doing things for the right reasons
- ensure you have made the end result compelling enough to want to achieve it
- find those things you like doing, those things that make you happy and do more of them

- focus on the positives in your daily life, as well as your goals and ambitions

Following on from this last point, be grateful for everything in your life – good and bad. The good things sustain you through the bad things. It is also worth remembering that the bad things are often there to help us learn an important lesson – they really are gifts in disguise, and if you can see them as good, everything will seem so much easier, better and more positive.

"When we think positively and imagine what we want, we risk disappointment; when we don't, we ensure it."

– Lana Limpert

BONUS QUESTION 11

> *"Happiness hides in life's small details.
> If you're not looking, it becomes invisible."*
>
> – Dr Joyce Brothers

Where Do You Find Happiness?

This is a question similar to 'What do I really want?' The answer is happiness is something only you can find. As I mentioned at the beginning of question 9, I personally think we all want two things – love and happiness – and you will find them both in places that are unique to you.

What I will do however, is try to give you some guidance, to help you avoid making common mistakes.

Your Idea of Happiness Is Unique To You

We are all unique, with our own individual likes, dislikes, dreams and ambitions. We like different hobbies, people and places, so the things you find that make you happy will be another person's pet hate.

This really leads me on to the number one mistake most of us make when looking for happiness:

You Are Looking In The Wrong Place!

Most of us start our search for happiness by looking outside of ourselves. We look for external things to make us happy – material things such as cars, wealth, partners etc.

So What Is the Problem With Looking Outside For Happiness?

Looking to external, outside factors to make you happy will ultimately lead to disappointment. The problems you will face are explained below.

Short-lived pleasure

Putting your happiness in material, external things will always lead to a short-lived pleasure. You may lose interest in these things, they could break or be damaged and your view of them may change (with or without other people's input).

Goal posts are always moving

What may seem a good source of happiness at the moment could change further down the line. If it's a place or event, the people running it may change the venue, attendees, layout etc. If you are putting your happiness into physical items or money, their value can change, you may decide you no longer have enough of them or you may even decide something else that is bigger, brighter and shinier may hold more value.

Situations change

Whether it is your personal situation or that of those people around you, situations are always changing. You may change or lose your job, your home or a family member – all of these will make you reassess your current situation. As a situation changes, your viewpoint may or may not change with it. Other things become more important – whilst other things will lose their importance.

Expectations change

The expectations you hold and those of people around you will change, depending on any of the above (as well as for other reasons).

So, What Is The Answer?

Ultimately, the only place you will find true happiness, as cliché as it sounds, is inside you. True happiness comes from a place of love; love for your family, gratitude for everything you have, love for your life and ultimately love for yourself.

By working on your confidence and self esteem you will have started not only a journey towards improving those two areas – but ultimately towards finding true happiness.

This Book has been designed to give you the first steps you can take towards loving yourself – it is your job to take action on these steps; as well as continuing your own journey. You will find the action steps relating to self confidence and self esteem in the following sections of this Book. Now is the perfect time for you to start implementing them.

I can also offer you further help and advice through my new 6 week online course *'Blast Your Self Confidence & Esteem To New Levels'*. The details of this course are available under the 'Further Help' section at the end of this Book, along with a list of books and websites that will help you along the way – so make sure you check out that section too!

"Happiness is inward and not outward; and so it does not depend on what we have, but on what we are."

– Henry Van Dyke

SECTION 2 – ASSESSING YOUR CURRENT SITUATION

In this section we will be using the insights you have gained from Section 1, along with those that crop up in this section, to look at creating a more in-depth picture of the different areas in your life, as they are at this moment in time, along with those things that may be currently holding you back. We will also look understanding those things that are in your control, such as your thoughts and emotions and how they are created. This section therefore covers:

- Rating your current situation
- Discovering your core beliefs, along with those limiting ones
- Your self talk and repetitive thought patterns
- An overview of your emotions and those negative ones to be avoided
- Those things that make you stressed
- Facing up to your fears and how fear holds you back

So, grab a pen and some paper – and let's start getting practical!

CHAPTER 12

*"A question works because, unlike a statement which
requires you to obey,
a question requires you to think.
The mind seems to prefer to think, not to obey."*

– Nancy Kline

RATING YOUR CURRENT SITUATION

Before you can move forward, you need to have a complete plan in place.

This includes knowing where you are headed (which will be covered in Section 3) and knowing what you are moving forward from (in other words, what is your starting position?).

This information will enable you to compile your own goalposts along the way, to monitor your progress and your achievements.

To accurately assess your starting position, you need to look at all the areas in your life. These areas are:

- Health
- Money
- Family and friends
- Relationships
- Environment
- Personal growth
- Career
- Fun/recreation

Compile an Accurate View

Having an accurate view of your current situation helps you discover what really are the root causes of your self confidence and self esteem issues. Once established you will then be able to understand what areas really need working on.

So, grab a pen and some paper, and write a paragraph or two to describe each area, based on your current situation. To make it easier, I have given you a few questions below to help you know what the different areas cover and to come up with answers.

Health

- How good is your diet?
- Do you drink plenty of water each day?
- What are your eating habits? Do you have three meals a day? Do you eat with the family, or eat when hungry? Do you comfort eat? If so, when and for what reasons?
- Do you participate in any sports or other forms of fitness?
- What helps you to relax? Do you have time to relax? If not, what stops you – the children, work, motivation?
- How do you feel about your current body and weight?

Money

- How would you describe your financial situation?
- Do you currently work?
- Do you have savings?
- How do you view money? For example, do you see it as a way to get things you want or the route of all evil?
- How do you deal with financial decisions? For example, do you like making them? Do you make them on your own or with your partner? Does your partner have the final say?

- What was the last thing you bought just for you? When was this?

Family & Friends

- Describe your current situation – do you have lots of friends and family?
- How close are you to your immediate family?
- How would you describe your parents?
- What are the biggest benefits of having: a partner, children, family and friends?
- If you wanted to discuss a problem, who would you talk to?
- Who is guaranteed to cheer you up and make you laugh?
- How does each of your friends make you feel?
- What do you believe about having family and friends? (For example, do they help and support you or do you believe they hold you back?)
- What were your reasons for having a family of your own?

Relationships

- How does each of your immediate family make you feel? (your partner, children and parents)
- How do you get on with your neighbours?
- Name the good things that each of your immediate family give you (relating to emotions and feelings; for example stability, love, support, laughter, happiness, relaxation etc)
- Describe your relationship with your partner
- What are your feelings and thoughts about having a partner? What were your reasons for getting married/living with someone?

Environment
- How do you feel about your current home and neighbourhood?
- How would you describe your current environment – is it noisy, peaceful, calm, disorganised?
- How do you feel when you are in your home? Do you feel safe, peaceful, stressed, depressed?
- Are you a hoarder or a clearer? Do objects hold sentiment for you or remind you of particular events?
- Would you describe your home as a reflection of you and your family, if so, why?

Personal Growth
- Do you currently use any form of meditation or relaxation techniques?
- Name three things you have achieved that make you proud
- What do you think about your personal growth? Do you like reading inspirational books? Do you believe you have achieved all your personal growth or are there things you would still like to experience or adopt?
- What was the last thing you learnt? Do you complete a home study or college course? Did you work through a self development book?

Career
- What is your current work situation?
- How do you feel about your current job?
- What hours do you work?
- What are your relationships like with colleagues?
- What do you like about your current job?
- How does your work environment feel?
- How does your work make you feel?

Fun & Recreation
- What do you do for fun?
- Do you have any hobbies or go to any clubs or groups?
- Who do you like having fun with?
- When was the last time you had fun?

Describe You

Now, if you had to describe yourself to someone, what would you say? I want you to write a few paragraphs in answer to each of the following. Describe your:

- appearance
- positive and negative thoughts about you
- usual emotions (are you emotional or do you keep them under wraps)
- likes and dislikes
- talents and character traits
- what you are scared of
- what you worry about
- what you dream about

Take Your Time

Looking at your current situation and yourself can be quite revealing – and upsetting. It can leave you feeling a bit like a wrung out dishrag; depressed, down, upset and disheartened. **This is perfectly normal**, as you are facing the facts of your life as it stands at the moment – it can be quite an eye-opener – and quite a depressing one at that.

So give yourself time to settle your emotions a bit. Have a cup of tea, read a good book or magazine for half an hour or go for a walk. Remember that you are making positive steps to face up to your current situation and to move it (and you!) into a better, more positive space. You're doing great!

*"Curiosity will conquer fear
Even more than bravery will."*

– James Stephens

CHAPTER 13

> *"The most powerful thing you can do to change the world is to change your own beliefs about the nature of life, people and reality to something more positive...and begin to act accordingly."*
>
> – Shakti Gawain

In this chapter we will be looking at those areas that could potentially hold you back. For the sake of ease, I am going to call these areas 'gremlins' and we will be addressing how to deal with them in the 'Moving Forward' section. For now, we are going to look at them in greater detail.

Whilst reading Chapter 13 – 17, you may like to record your thoughts in a journal or on some paper. You can also spend a week on each of the following chapters, noticing your corresponding behaviours and recording your findings in your journal or in a notebook.

THE CORE BELIEFS YOU LIVE BY

What is your belief structure?

Your belief structure comprises of a core set of rules that you live your daily life by. They are made up of how and what you think and believe, along with why you think and believe what you do, about the world – and yourself. Basically, your beliefs are not fact; they are your opinions, ideas, judgements and assumptions, and all those principles and doctrines you consider to be true.

These beliefs are what govern how you think, talk and act – how you comprehend and analyse any situation or event – and how you react as a result. You have beliefs about everything; from how you see yourself right through to politics and religion. Your beliefs define how you process and store information as it comes through your conscious mind, ensuring you find data to back up your view of the world.

How Beliefs are Made

As mentioned at the start of this section, beliefs are not fact – they are actually our personal opinions, with expectations attached. We start formulating our beliefs from an early age, usually inheriting them from our parents, siblings, media and other authority figures. So your upbringing will have a major impact on your beliefs. For example, If your mother stayed at home whilst your father worked, and you were frequently told 'wait until your father gets home' when you had been naughty, then you will have deducted several possible beliefs from this:

- mums (females) stay home
- dads (males) bring in the money
- dads (males) are the authority
- dads (males) are the disciplinarians
- mums (females) are the peace keepers
- mums (females) are meek and mild
- dads (males) are strong and tough
- dads (males) word is law
- mums (females) lower than dad (males)

As we grew older, outside influences and people helped to shape our beliefs. We still looked for acceptance from others, so people who caused us to have any doubts about this would influence how we acted – thus leading us to live our lives via someone else's viewpoint. An example of this would be if you hung around with 'the wrong crowd' or the 'in crowd'; you would frequently have surrendered your own beliefs to adopt those rules or beliefs of the majority.

Advertising plays on the fact that we all want to be accepted. Advertisers will use different tactics to get you to change your view (or belief) about a product, by making you feel like you are not 'normal', 'may be missing out' or 'in some way inadequate' in an effort to get you to buy their products.

How We Use Beliefs

We look for evidence to back up our belief structure, as we go about our daily lives. So for example, if you have 'you must be honest' as one of your beliefs, and your job involves you telling white lies to you customers – you will be going against one of your core beliefs – and if this is continued over a long period of time – your happiness will be affected.

We filter out any sensory data taken from the environment that doesn't match our beliefs by favouring data that supports and confirms them. We build the strength of a belief by compiling lots of confirming data – although this causes us to generalise and distort our view of the world. For example, you are upset or angry because your husband is late home. You say it's because he's late, but you may actually be thinking it's because he may be cheating on you – which has its roots in a belief that he doesn't love you anymore.

Beliefs also motivate us, as we all tend to work towards getting more things we consider as valuable – whether that is time with your family, time alone or career related. This will lead you to filter out anything that you consider as less valuable.

How Beliefs Affect Your Feelings

It is quite common to reach a certain age or point in your life and feel like you are no longer in control. Emotionally, you can feel lost, frustrated, upset and stagnant. We can feel we have lost control through illness, trauma, changes in our lives or burn-out – but the most common reason is actually unconsciously giving our control over to another person.

When we get married, move in with a partner or have there is a need to compromise and adapt. After all, you are sharing your life with another person. The problems arise when you start compromising on too many of your beliefs. Over a period of time you have adapted so much that you feel you are no longer 'you'. This can leave you feeling out of control, pointless and insignificant. You feel depressed and disappointed, uninteresting, and feel as though you are taken for granted – leaving you feeling resentful and hurt.

Limiting Beliefs

As mentioned above, beliefs have the ability to make us feel negative as well as positive. Limiting beliefs are those beliefs that make us feel bad, inadequate and inferior. They hold us back from realising our full potential and prevent us from doing things we want to do. A lot of the negative 'facts' we have about ourselves are actually the result of one or more of our limiting beliefs. As a well-known saying goes: whether you believe you can or can't – you are probably right.

> *"Within you right now is the power to do things*
> *you never dreamed possible.*
> *This power becomes available to you*
> *just as soon as you can change your beliefs."*
>
> – Dr Maxwell Maltz

CHAPTER 14

*"Your opponent, in the end, is never really the player on the other side of the net,
or the swimmer in the next lane, or the team on the other side of the field,
or even the bar you must high-jump.
You opponent is yourself, your negative internal voices, your level of determination."*

– Grace Lichtenstein

OUR SELF TALK

The Power of Words

There's an old saying "sticks and stones may break my bones, but names will never hurt me." Anyone who has been on the receiving end of negative words will be first to admit that words do actually hurt. Sometimes they even have the ability to create wounds that never seem to heal.

We also know how positive words can lift us to new heights; make us feel special and invincible. They can give us much needed strength and motivate us forward. This doesn't just apply to words we receive from others – it also applies to the words we ourselves use – when talking to others and when talking to ourselves.

The phrases you use when talking to others, will tend to highlight your low self esteem. You have voiced them so often that they have become habit. It is at this stage that, they are so habitually used you become unaware of even saying them. Phrases used to constantly put you down are common, such as:

- I'm sorry
- I'm so stupid/dumb etc
- I'm useless
- Why am I so pathetic, weak, feeble etc
- I'm fine, don't worry about me (or don't worry about it)
- I look a mess

You are voicing them to reaffirm that you are correct in your self assessment. It is important that all your beliefs are correct – even those ones that have a negative influence on your life; such as 'I am worthless or useless'. These comments are also said to pre-empt other people saying them first. This is used as a defence tactic; to protect your feelings from being hurt by others – however, in doing so, you are actually causing much of the damage to yourself!

Self Talk

This is the dialogue running through your head. It is the wording we use when talking to ourselves; to describe experiences, challenges, other people and ourselves. In other words – it is our daily vocabulary. Your self talk helps you to filter your life; the people you meet, how you communicate with others, the events in your life – it can make your life colourful or varying shades of grey. Self talk has the ability to push you towards success, help you heal, make you laugh – or cause you discomfort and pain, cause you to cry and destroy things in your life. Your words and thoughts build your beliefs and actions.

Negative Inner Talk

This is one of the most destructive symptoms of low self esteem – quite often because we don't even notice the wording we are using. The negative wording is allowed free rein to play on 'auto repeat' in our mind and, as stated above, creates deep rooted beliefs and unnoticed habits.

Your brain has a staggering average 70,000 thoughts a day – with an approximate 80% of those being negative. That's an incredible average amount of 56,000 negative thoughts a day! You cannot hope to be consciously aware of that amount of thought each day, so the vast majority of those thoughts are left to run riot in your mind – rooting and confirming those negative thought patterns further inside your brain, the more you find evidence to confirm they are true.

How We Build Our Thought Patterns

Someone may have made a passing comment about your appearance or your inability to do something that tweaked a negative response in you. Your brain links your response and reaction to an emotion, making that comment more important to remember – after all, we don't like the feeling of any negative emotion. That statement is then stored with that emotion attached.

Next time you feel that emotion, or hear something similar said to you, your brain links it with that negative emotion again. Before long, you have a pattern developing that says 'people comment about my abilities/appearance: I feel bad: I feel bad because I cannot do xyz/my appearance is 'abnormal' in some way: resulting in me feeling bad.

We continually look for data to reinforce our negative or positive opinions. Data with an emotion attached will be at the front of the queue, so any strong negative (or positive) data will be there. If you have a negative opinion of your appearance, your brain will focus on things to back this up and it will filter out any positive things as irrelevant or unimportant. Whether you think or say a negative comment about your appearance – it will store this as relevant. If someone else says something negative about your appearance – it will store this with the other relevant pieces of information, thus reinforcing your negative opinion.

> *"Don't listen to whiners. Including yourself."*
>
> – Unknown

CHAPTER 15

> *"Control your emotions or your emotions will control your life... especially the negative ones."*
>
> – Unknown

YOUR EMOTIONS

What Are Emotions?

Emotion (also called feeling) is a fundamental trait associated with being human. They aid in our survival, give our lives depth and colour and differentiate us from others. It is an instinctive state of mind we experience from our circumstances, mood, personality and relationships with other people. Emotions are also associated to motivation – they can energise and direct our focus, whilst motivating your to act a certain way – positively and negatively.

Experiences such as love and hate, fear and anger, joy and grief are all emotions. Whereas emotions are short-lived and usually in reaction to a specific event, our moods are more general feelings that can last for a longer length of time, such as happiness and sadness, contentment and frustration.

We monitor and regulate our social interactions with others by unconsciously learning to read their body language, we then apply past experiences to determine what they are feeling and how we should react as a result.

Although scientists cannot agree on what emotions are, or how they should measure them, they do agree that they have the following parts:

- Subjective feelings (how you experience feelings)
- Physiological responses (how your body reacts to the feeling)
- Expressive behaviour (how you show feelings)

The subjective feelings, or how we react to the emotion, is the most difficult to measure or describe as they cannot be observed – and each person will have their own interpretation and description of that emotion and feeling.

How Emotions Affect You

As already mentioned, emotions (or feelings) will affect you in different ways, however all emotions will trigger physiological responses such as:

- pounding heart
- sweating
- blood rushing to face

Our body language allows us to give an outward sign that we are experiencing emotion. These expressive behaviours include:

- flushed face
- muscle tension
- facial expression
- tone of voice
- rapid breathing
- restlessness
- and even fainting

Internally, your body releases the hormone adrenaline. This prepares your body to react ie the 'fight or flight' response. When we low or unhappy we will suffer similar responses, as they both affect our daily life in the same way. To recap, these end results will include:

- reduced ability to cope with day-to-day life
- difficulty in holding down a job or relationship
- withdrawing from having contact with other people (including friends and family)
- obsessive thoughts and repeated behaviour patterns (such as endlessly washing your hands)
- feeling frightened and vulnerable
- stressed and tense
- stagnant, no energy spirit is trapped – no sense of connection
- closed to new possibilities
- weak personal power
- no defence against challenges life may throw your way
- feeling like you have nowhere to turn

How We Learn To Associate Our Memories

We often link our emotions to particular memories - good and bad. This linking process would have started from when you were a small child, right through to your adult self. If you suffered any kind of physical, emotional or sexual trauma (particularly as a child), the emotions you may have felt as a result would have been too overwhelming to understand or deal with.

But it isn't just as a result of negative memories. You may have had parents who loved you so much that they wrapped you in cotton wool or smothered you too much. You may have been a highly sensitive child who had a vivid imagination; maybe you felt misunderstood, shamed or neglected. How your parents treated you (good and bad) as well as how you dealt with the emotions you had as a result, will have determined how you learnt to associate your feelings to memories. All the different scenarios you went through would have made you learn to embrace or hide your emotions.

We learn how to numb out the pain caused by extreme emotions – usually by learning to stash it in our mind; thinking rather than feeling. We also learn other ways to numb out the pain by using food, drugs, alcohol – and it all shapes us into the person we now are. Maybe you learnt to overachieve or try to make sure everything was perfect – in order to keep busy. Alternatively, you may have learnt to live in a make believe world to avoid being in your own body or used anger as a way of covering your upset and feelings of helplessness.

Women are very good at focusing on others rather than facing their own feelings and emotions. We try to be there for others, absorbing their feelings rather than facing our own pain.

As adults, our emotions are quite often a result of our thoughts. We cause a lot of our own pain by judging ourselves; in effect abandoning ourselves to the negativity and self judgement we produce every day. In thinking negative thoughts (such as 'I am useless' or 'I am not worth…') we cause ourselves to feel depressed and anxious. This can often lead us to develop our own ways of dealing with these feelings, with anger and/or obsessive behaviour and habits, resulting in Obsessive Compulsive Disorder (OCD).

The Negative Emotions That Can Stop You In Your Tracks

Holding onto negative emotions and their associated memories can stop you from growing and developing. They get buried in our subconscious mind and have a major impact on how we live our lives. These emotions can leave you feeling permanently on edge and oversensitive, acting hostile and sarcastic and in the long term can become a barrier in your relationships – sometimes even causing the relationship to break down completely. The main negative emotions are listed below.

Guilt

We are very good at carrying several layers of guilt around with us, sometimes on a daily basis. We feel guilty for going to work and leaving our children with a childminder, but feel guilty if we don't work. We want to spend time with our children – then feel guilty if we want time on our own or want to have time alone with our partners.

Other people can also try to make us feel guilty, adding to our guilt trip. Our parents can make us feel guilty for not calling/spending time with them; ditto our friends. Our partners may lay on the guilt if we don't want to cook, clean or dress and act a certain way. Then, when at work, we feel guilty if we want our break or lunch during a busy day, or if we cannot stay late to finish a project.

Resentment

Resentment is the bitterness you feel over a real or imagined wrong doing. It is usually aimed at someone who you consider to have a higher status than you. It is usually sparked by an injustice or humiliation including negative treatment, discrimination or jealousy and envy.

In relationships it is easy to feel as though you are being taken advantage of (by your partner or children) and you can feel as though your efforts and achievements are going unrecognised. This can lead you to emotionally rejecting the other person, belittling them and even deliberately embarrassing them.

Revenge

Looking to get even with someone who wronged you will get you nowhere – except stressed and angry (not to mention the effect it has on your mental and physical health). The fact of the matter is that the person involved has probably continued living their life and forgotten whatever happened. Holding onto revengeful thoughts is inhibiting both your growth and your ability to move on with your life.

Anger

Anger is a natural response to any perceived threat, however if it is allowed to fester, it will sap your energy and weigh you down. It stops you from forgiving and moving forward.

Sadness

Sadness again, is a natural response to an event or situation. Time does heal and sadness will dissipate at its own rate. However if you are holding onto it, causing it to linger longer than needed, then you are really doing yourself no favours. Feeling sad does not change what happened, however seeking peace of mind will enable you to move your life on.

*"Reacting is an emotional reflex.
Response requires thought."*

– Gail Pursell Elliott

CHAPTER 16

"Stress won't go away if unresolved conflict exists. It's like painting primer over rotting wood."

– Scott Morton

THE STRESS IN YOUR LIFE

What is Stress?

Everything about today's world is fast – we work fast (often with shorter deadlines), travel fast and rush everywhere; we even socialise fast (via social media). Living such a fast-paced live has made stress a huge problem in our everyday lives and our work environments. If it isn't managed, stress can lead onto more serious illnesses.

We all know that worrying excessively about something will cause stress, but your body will react stressfully to any change – good or bad. When problems or events (physical and psychological; imagined or real) keep our body at a heightened level of alertness, stress is created. Stress can be caused by any number of things including:

- Promotion/demotion
- Redundancy/starting a new job
- Being in work/being out of work
- Finances
- Moving home
- Illness (your own and of those around you)
- Late nights and/or early starts

- Problems and issues we face in our day-to-day life

As you can see, different extremes of situation, as well as normal events, can cause stress; basically anything that causes a change in your lifestyle or health. It is much more than 'just' worrying about something; it can be caused by events or situations that make you feel happy or sad, physical as well as emotional (like worrying about something). We can be carrying an enormous amount of stress around with us – without even realising it!

How Stress Affects You

When life is running smoothly your brain produces chemicals like serotonin, to keep up with your normal daily demands and expectations. If your brain is put under too much stress, it will struggle to cope with producing those calming chemicals fast enough. Your nerve centres become distressed and your brain enters a state of chemical imbalance – you're overstressed. Being stressed will leave you feeling:

- Overwhelmed
- Exhausted
- Lethargic
- Depressed and anxious
- Unable to cope
- Unhappy

You may also suffer from:

- Too much or too little sleep
- Aches and pains
- Lacking any sparkle
- Skin and stomach problems

Fear can also be a factor for creating stress. We will be discussing what fear is and how it affects you in the following chapter.

"It takes as much stress to be a success as it does to be a failure."

– Emilio James Trujillo

CHAPTER 17

*"You can conquer almost any fear if you will only make up your mind to do so.
For remember, fear doesn't exist anywhere except in the mind."*

– Dale Carnegie

FACING YOUR FEARS

Fear is Natural

Fear is a pre-programmed emotion we all have; it is an instinct we have in response to perceived danger. Fear also serves to sharpen our mind, to encourage us to focus on the task at hand. Adrenaline and the hormone cortisol are released into our blood stream which then causes our body to react – we will select either our 'fight' or 'flight' response to the situation.

In survival fear is a necessary emotion – problems arise when our 'flight or fight' response kicks in unnecessarily for example, with phobias. Anxiety sufferers fear future-orientated events; phobia sufferers fear something that cannot actually hurt them, and panic is us having a physical response to an irrational or unrealistic fear. Usually our initial startle response will subside once we realise we are under no threat.

If our panic and fears are left to fester and grow, or our startle response doesn't subside, then fears can make each day a struggle. You want to move forward but fear has a hold on you; leaving you unsure which direction to turn for help. Some days you're even unsure which direction is actually the right one for what you want to achieve.

When tackling your fears, there are three points you need to remember:

- everyone has them
- you can't run away from them
- they need to be tackled head on – no matter how strong they are

How We Get Them?

Fears are like beliefs – they originate from how you interpret an event, situation or object. Our worries and anxieties about a particular 'thing' overwhelm us, leading us to distort our perception of reality. We link an emotion (usually fear of upset) to whatever is around at that moment we feel it. For example, you could have two people walk into a dark room; one person may be affected by the dark, whilst the other person may be affected by the spider they spotted in the corner.

As children we struggle to understand the responses we have to certain situations and events. We may not have been able to rationalise the fear we felt – this is especially relevant when dealing with separation from those people in authority (our parents, childminders, school teachers etc). Overactive imaginations (if left to run riot) created monsters in the dark, burglars in the garden and tragic events that could permanently prevent our parents from returning and leaving us alone and unloved.

These usually dispel as we get older, however if other events added to our worries we could easily carry these fears into our adult lives.

How Do Fears Affect Us?

Panic and fear can affect you in different ways. There are physical and emotional symptoms, caused by the rush of the stress hormone cortisol and the adrenaline in our body. These cause our body to react in different ways including:

- stress & tension
- trembling
- feeling tearful and irritable
- pounding heartbeat
- chest pains
- churning stomach
- muscle tension
- feeling sick and/or faint
- headache
- tiredness/difficulty sleeping
- sweating
- Procrastination – we all know this one! We put off doing what needs to be done; especially when it will bring us closer to our desired end result.
- Overwhelm – this is the opposite of procrastination. You have so much information around you (whether that is all those things you want to achieve, or the large amount of steps involved) you just don't know where to start.

The Big Fears

These fears are the big ones that tend to affect women – especially during relationships (with partners and family) and whilst raising children:

- fear of failure

- fear of success – this is actually harder to spot than fear of failure – and harder to eradicate
- fear of pain
- fear of rejection

You may argue that there are others that aren't on this list however I believe that most fears can be traced back to these four – although you could actually break all four down into fear of pain or rejection! All of these fears have the ability to stop action in its tracks, leaving us unable to make decisions in case of rejection or a negative outcome.

Fear of Failure

Most women are more emotional than the men in their lives. I will be helping you to deal with your emotions in a separate section of this book; however those emotions often lead us to worry more – about other people and ourselves. We worry whether we are living up to other people's ideals – especially our partners.

Quite often we can worry excessively about how we look to others, letting them down and making ourselves look 'dumb' or 'stupid', so rather than run the risk of failing – we just don't start at all. This can easily lead us to avoiding relationships altogether as we are so scared of it going wrong.

Fear of Success

Quite often we look at improving our current relationships (or ourselves) by studying various self help/development books and courses and then try to implement changes in our life. If your life doesn't change (or even gets worse) you could be subconsciously sabotaging your efforts due to a fear of success. This is also the case if you start the changes full of enthusiasm – but stop putting in the effort when nearing completion.

Women are good at settling for less than they feel they are capable of achieving, or than they feel they deserve. They fear what will happen if they do succeed in aiming (and reaching) something higher. The worry revolves around them changing and what other people will a) think of that, b) losing people as a result and c) how life will change generally as a result.

Fear of Pain
Fear of pain is quite a biggie – it covers everything from physical pain to emotional pain. Anyone who has had a relationship breakup will know how painful it is. We will do almost anything to prevent it. Therefore this fear will include everything from a relationship breakup, right through to the pain felt when your child yells something nasty about you in the heat of an argument. It is the reason why we stay in unhappy relationships, put up with our children's bad behaviour and why we spend a lot of time stressed! Fear of pain is often intertwined with the final big fear – the fear of rejection.

Fear of Rejection
We already know rejection hurts – this is why this fear is intertwined with the fear of pain. Rejection however, is so much more than our partner rejecting us – it includes other people we are involved with too.

When you were little, you listened to your parents. If you did something wrong and got told off – you felt the pain. You also feared you were being rejected too. You feared they would stop loving you. Children watching their parents' divorce will often fear they will be rejected by one or the other. We take fear of rejection as a withdrawal of love.

Summary

Now you have an accurate overview of your current situation, as well as understanding those things you have control of, it is time to start working on your own personal action plan.

I want you to re-read what you have written about your current situation and see what you have gleaned from it as a result. See if you can separate sections of it under the headings of 'beliefs', 'emotions', 'fears', 'stress' and 'negative thoughts'.

Once that is done, we can look at ways to solve these, along with creating our action plan of steps for moving our confidence and esteem onwards and upwards!

"Don't fear failure so much that you refuse to try new things.
The saddest summary of a life contains three descriptions:
could have, might have, and should have."

– Louis E Boone

SECTION 3 – MOVING FORWARD; SOLVING THOSE PROBLEMS RELATED TO LOW SELF CONFIDENCE AND SELF ESTEEM

In this section we will be asking those questions that will help you create your own personal action plan. This is broken down as follows:

- Firstly in Chapter 18, we will be covering some important points to remember when working on your self confidence and self esteem. Some of these may seem easy, however they are crucial to your success
- Chapter 19 is all about the basics of goal setting and ensuring you stay motivated
- Chapter 20 is where you formulate your action plan!
- Remember those gremlins we looked at earlier that were in your control? Those little gremlins are what can potentially hold you back, so in Chapter 21 we will be looking at changing your beliefs and thoughts, getting a handle on your emotions, managing stress and solving your fears – anything that may hold you up from completing your action plan.

CHAPTER 18

*"Here's the risk you take when you change: that people you've been involved with
won't like the new you. But other people who do will come along."*

– Lisa Alther

MOVING FORWARD

A lot of the time, we blame our parents for problems we have as adults. Yes, our upbringing plays a huge part in the basic building blocks of our confidence and esteem – <u>but</u> those building blocks are not so deeply rooted that we are stuck with them forever. We alone, are responsible for making the decision to stick with those blocks or change them for something else.

We all have the ability, <u>at any time</u>, to decide whether we are happy, or not, with our current lot.

The main things to remember before you look at improving your confidence and esteem:

- Take ownership
- It can be changed for the better
- Decide whether you want to stay as you are, or improve
- You can start from anywhere
- You only need to take small steps
- You have to do some form of action!
- Reward yourself for each accomplishment

We will be looking at these in greater detail in this chapter. The following chapters will cover further information on moving forward as follows:

Chapter 19 will cover:
- Details on how to set achievable, manageable goals, without causing overwhelm
- Tips to help you keep motivated and on track

Chapter 20 will cover:
- Survey and plan – this is where you compile your in-depth action plan!

Tip:

As you go through this chapter it is worth having a pen some paper handy to make notes of any areas you may need to work on, for example who you blame for your situation and/or what the benefits are for not changing your confidence and esteem.

So, without further delay, let's look at those points to be covered in this chapter, in greater detail.

Important Things to Remember

Take Ownership

As mentioned in the opening paragraph above, the first step towards improving your confidence and self esteem is to actually take ownership of the problem.

We spend a lot of time blaming other people and outside factors for our problems and issues. Now, I'm not saying they don't play a part – as they do – however, until you decide to face the fact that YOU have this problem, you will always have it.

By blaming it on other people and outside factors you keep that low confidence at arm's length; leaving it as something outside factors and other people have ultimate control of. When you face it as a problem you have control of, you take ownership of it along with that control – so it then becomes something you can control and alter as you see fit.

It Can Be Changed For the Better

Now you have claimed ownership of your low self confidence and esteem, you can now decide that it can be altered – as it is in your control. You alone, can make the decision that you would like to improve those areas of your personality for the better. The ball, as they say, is in your court.

Decide Whether You Want to Stay as You Are or Improve

Simply ask yourself: 'am I happy being this way? Am I happy being shy/scared/lonely etc?' In truth, 99.9% of you will say 'no. I am not', however this is only part of this step.

The next question to ask yourself is: 'what do I get from being this way?' Write your answers down. This part of the process can seem like a step backwards, as you are focusing on the reasons NOT to change your confidence or esteem levels. The fact of the matter is you are getting something beneficial from being low in confidence and esteem. Until you faced with the benefits of staying put, you will find it harder to move forward.

For example, some of the benefits of staying put could include:

- I don't get hurt (I feel safe)
- I don't have to hang around with people I don't know (I avoid confrontation, disappointment, embarrassment etc)

- I don't have to make any big decisions (I can avoid taking ownership if it goes wrong, I avoid looking bad, I avoid potential disappointment, I avoid disappointing others)
- I don't have to live up to much (I avoid the risk of disappointing others and/or myself)

So, as you can see, the benefits will often highlight the root issues of your low confidence and esteem – quite often, it will boil down to either a fear of failure/success and/or a fear of looking bad/other people being disappointed in you.

You Can Start From Anywhere

The good thing about building your self confidence and self esteem is that you can start the moment you decide to start, from whatever place your life is currently in.

You don't have to wait for any outside factor or any other person. It doesn't depend on your grades, education, job situation or the weather! Roughly translated: there's no reason why you can't start now! Your first step is simply to make the decision – the next step is to know in what direction you want to take that next step!

Hold your horses though!

So far, we have covered pretty much every area of assessing your current situation, through to getting a plan in place. You are probably eager to get started on taking those first steps; you may even want to skim through the next paragraphs as you have all the 'important' stuff already covered – right?

Wrong! There are three more important things to remember that we haven't actually covered yet. The following points may sound small and hardly worth bothering with – however, they play a fundamentally important part in whether you succeed or fail in your quest to improve your self confidence and self esteem. So let's look at them in greater detail.

You Only Need to Take Small Steps

Trying to run before you can walk is pointless – we all know that, however it can be tempting to look at your action plan and say to yourself 'right, I'm going to dump all my toxic friends, get rid of my entire wardrobe, rack up my credit card by buying new clothes, paying for a new haircut, booking a one-way ticket to wherever I want to live ..... Stop! Slow down!

As tempting as all that might sound and I applaud your 'go-get-them' attitude, however, going in with all guns blazing will not only burn you out, but will also blow the safety blanket you've built with your current situation, to smithereens. You don't have to do it all in one hit (before you lose your nerve!).

Taking things one step at a time will be kinder to you, those around you and, most importantly, it will ensure that the changes you make will stick. If you want an example, look at those faddy diets that we women go on. You know, the ones that promise you will lose a stone in two weeks – if you live on celery sticks and green tea or some other weird combination. It may work short-term, but when you come back to the real world of normal eating, you'll overcompensate, eat everything you've been craving – and end up back at what feels 'safe'; your original weight (plus a bit more).

So, look at your list of steps and make sure they are broken down into easy, manageable small steps.

You Have to do Some Form of Action!

Now you may have the best intentions in the world. You'll read this book (and others) from cover to cover and even gone on the corresponding websites. You may have added a few other interesting books on self-confidence and self-esteem to your Amazon wish list, purchased another and even added more interesting looking websites to your favourites – but don't get lulled into a false sense of security.

The fact is there will always be a new book or website that catches your eye. With so much information available at your fingertips, you could complete Google searches until the cows come home. But at some stage you are going to have to stop searching for the next bright shiny objects and actually start doing something towards achieving your end result!

Any goal you want to achieve, whether it be connected to sport, work or self improvement (such as building your confidence or esteem) will involve you putting in some form of effort. A problem a lot of us make, especially when related to the self improvement field, is to read every book on a particular subject – and then be disappointed when we are still in our starting situations. You have to follow up your research with some actual action!

Select Your Action Step Now!

When you have completed your Action Plan in Chapter 20, you will have a completed list of small steps you can take, to get you from your starting position and moving towards your end destination. You have to then make a decision as to which one you could focus on. You then have to decide when you are going to complete the action steps involved. Can you start it today? If not, when can you? When are you aiming to finish it by?

You've made the decision, now act on it!

Reward Yourself for Each Accomplishment

This may seem like it's of no real consequence but, this is going to be one of the things that will help keep you motivated.

Your rewards don't have to be big – but they do have to be something special for you. The size of reward can also be tailored to the size of the step, for example: if your goal is to lose those negative friends for good; the reward for achieving this could be having a meal out with your new friends. If you were working on a section of this goal (like limiting phone contact) you could call another positive friend to meet you for coffee.

As we are all unique, we will all be motivated by different things. You may find money motivating, so give your goals a monetary value for the reward. If you're motivated by good food, use this as your motivation (it doesn't have to mean expensive meals out – you could buy a good quality chocolate bar etc).

So find what motivates you and use these things as your rewards.

"Change. It has the power to uplift, to heal, to stimulate, surprise, open new doors, bring fresh experience and create
excitement in life. Certainly it is worth the risk."

- Leo Buscaglia

CHAPTER 19

"If you aim at nothing, you'll hit it."

– Unknown

GOAL SETTING & MOTIVATION

Basics of Goal Setting

There are entire books dedicated to goal setting, however in this chapter, I will be giving you a brief overview of how to set goals in such a way that you are more likely to achieve them. This is followed by a section on staying motivated – essential to keeping you on track and achieving those targets you have set.

Why Set Goals?

Many people are unhappy with their current position. Whether this relates to your confidence, esteem, career or life in general, we all have things we would like to improve or achieve. We imagine how things would be if we had those things in our lives; achieved those ambitions; lived that other life.

Setting goals is a way to focus where you actually want to put your energies, with regards to improving your situation. Setting goals (accurately) will enable you to see where you are headed; how you want to get there and how long it will take. It takes your dreams from imagination to reality.

Goals Versus Wishes

We are all guilty of setting New Year resolutions; vague 'wishes' of things we'd like to achieve however, by February most of us have broken those resolutions – purely because they weren't actually goals. A wish is something you would like to have; a goal is a step-by-step list of actions to actually achieve what you want.

How to Set Goals That You Will Accomplish

Setting a goal isn't just about writing down something you want to achieve, and then taking action. There are specific things that you need look at <u>before</u> you start on the journey, to ensure you are successful and will actually achieve what you set out to accomplish.

The steps below should be followed for each goal you want to set, to ensure ultimate success.

Be Specific

Each of your goals needs to be specific. Saying you want to be more confident, lose weight or join a club isn't specific enough. How exactly do you want to be more confident? Does it mean you want to do a speech in front of people, or do you want to be able to voice your opinion to your partner or colleagues? How much weight do you want to lose? What club do you want to join? Get as specific as you can.

Realistic

Be realistic in what you can achieve, along with the timescales you set. You might want to host a party for 500 people; but setting a timescale of 2 weeks is totally unrealistic. You may want to have enough confidence to meet the man of your dreams (needs to be more specific!), however wanting to settle down by next year, with this guy you haven't yet met, may be a bit unrealistic.

When setting goals relating to any weight loss, remember that you can comfortably lose 2-3 lbs a week. So stating a goal that involves you losing 2 stone in a month is not going to be realistic – and probably bad for your health.

It is also worth remembering that goals involving other people in your life may not be realistic (unless they have the same goal). It's easy to set a goal involving your partner or children, however you may be left disappointed if they are not aiming for the same thing. Instead of setting a goal like 'I want my husband to top nagging me', you would be better saying 'I want to stay calm when my husband voices his opinion.' You can then make this more specific and achievable by writing a set of actions you can complete.

What are the Obstacles?

If you know what the obstacles are, you can overcome them before they get in the way of you achieving your goal. Sometimes this is a case of sitting your partner or children down and explaining to them what you want to achieve and why. Maybe finances will be an obstacle – in that case you would make getting a job or saving a set amount of money an earlier goal on your list.

What Resources Do You Have?

What do you have to help you achieve your goals? Do you have a friend or colleague that can help you or introduce you to people of influence? Do you possess the skill and character traits needed to achieve your goal (or do you need to plan these into your action steps)? Do you have the time and/or finances at your disposal?

Why do you Want Achieve This Goal?

Knowing your reasons for planning this particular goal will ensure you are achieving something you want – not someone else. If the words 'I should' or 'I ought to' crop up when discussing your goal, you need to look at the reasons why you feel this way. Is it because that is how you envisage someone else would act to achieve this goal; or is it because you are aiming for a goal you feel other people would expect you to achieve?

Keep Positive

All goals must be stated in a positive way. Instead of using 'I don't want', change it to 'I do want'. You also want to ensure you are going in a forward and upward direction, not taking a step backwards in your life or situation.

Be Passionate!

You have to have a passion or desire for what you want to achieve, otherwise you won't complete it. Passion is the driving force behind your actions, and what will leave you fulfilled once that goal is reached. Desiring that end result is what will stop you from getting distracted, and keep you from getting discouraged.

Plan Your Goals

To avoid feeling overwhelmed, you must plan your goals. By breaking the goal down into manageable action steps, you focus on the smaller task at hand rather than getting disheartened by what still needs to be done.

Time Limit

As mentioned earlier, you have to be realistic with your timescale. You also have to actually set a time limit. 'Some day' or 'one day' are not timescales; they are pipedreams that will never be accomplished. You have to have an end date in mind to enable you to plan effectively; to add that sense of urgency and motivation to what you are doing.

What is the End Result?

What is the end result of what you want to achieve? How will you know when you have achieved it? This is similar to the 'being specific' step mentioned earlier. Saying your end result is better confidence or a healthier self esteem isn't specific enough. How will you know when you have reached them? What will it look like? How will you act?

What are the Consequences?

If you don't achieve your goal what are the consequences? People are usually motivated away from something or towards something. Which one are you? Use this to your advantage when goal setting by using either reward or consequences – or both – to motivate your goals.

Write Them Down

Writing your goals down helps cement them in your mind. Seeing what you want to achieve on paper, in front of you will help keep you motivated as well as creating a visual point of reference for what you have achieved. So, make a note of them.

Picture it

Visualising what your goal looks like, as well as how you will act once achieved, brings your desires to life. As mentioned in the 'visualisation' chapter, your brain doesn't know the difference between what is vividly imagined and what is real. So, use this to fool your mind into thinking you have already achieved it – so it will be easy to achieve it again.

Adaptable

Be open to alternative ways of achieving your goals. You may have a certain set of steps on how to reach your end result, but a better, faster way may become visible. This also applies to what your actual goal is – a better outcome may present itself to you.

Put in the Effort
Be willing to put in the effort and time for your goals. If you are easily swayed to leave your action step for something unrelated – you may want to re-visit your reasons for wanting to achieve this goal in the first place.

Reward
Make sure you are rewarding yourself along the way to achieving your goals, as well as once you have achieved them. This helps to keep you motivated and on the right track. If you completed an action step, no matter how small it was, reward your achievement.

You may be surrounded by people who pick holes in your goals or who try to discourage you. If this is the case, it may be worth you creating an affirmation linked to your goal. This way you can constantly reinforce the fact to yourself that your goal is real and achievable. We discuss affirmations in Section 4.

Staying Motivated

We looked at staying motivated whilst answering question 10, however I have reiterated and expanded on those details below, for anyone who may have skipped straight to this section.

Possible Causes For Struggling With Motivation

In order to be positive about something you need to be able to see a positive, happy outcome at the end. Whether you are working on goals related to your personal life, career or personal development, you need to have an overwhelming reason to reach your end target. So, with that in mind, let's look at the possible causes for struggling to stay positive.

No goal or plan

If you rushed ahead with trying to complete changes in your life without a plan of action, then this is the most obvious reason for you struggling to stay motivated. We need to know where we are headed to give us something to get motivated about. We also need to know we are working for a reason. Whether that reason is financial or personal, you need to get clear on why you are doing something – and for what reason.

Another part of this is planning. As the well-known saying goes – 'If you fail to plan, you plan to fail'. As with any goal setting, if you know the start and end places, you can compile a set of steps to get from one to the other.

Wrong goal

Look at the reason why you want to achieve what you want to are aiming for. If you are going into it for the wrong reasons or it may cause distress or upset to people you care about, then maybe that goal isn't right for you.

Whilst looking at your reasons you may realise you're actually doing it either for other people or because of other people. You will struggle to stay motivated and positive if you are heading for an end result you don't even want.

Not enough stimulation

Another reason you may be struggling to stay positive is you aren't motivated enough to stay positive. If this is the case, then you need to remind yourself what you will gain and achieve from whatever you are doing. Imagine the end result, whether it's a new job or a new you, picture it in glorious Technicolor, use all your senses and make it look big, bright and colourful.

Focusing on the negative

As mentioned in earlier chapters, having your focus on the wrong thing will not help you stay positive. If you are focusing on the negativity around you, it will drag you down – whether that is people or situations and places. Switch your focus to the positives; your outcome, friends and family, compliments, nice weather etc – anything to increase your motivation.

Steps To Help You Stay Motivated

Knowing what you want to achieve and making steps to achieve it, should be enough to keep you motivated. If however you are struggling to keep motivated, you may want to take a fresh look at the areas below.

Check You Have a Plan

If you already have a plan in place, check that it is achievable. It is also worth checking that you are not overwhelming yourself by trying to do too much at once. Do you need to break down your steps into smaller ones?

Reassess Your Reasons

Ensure you want to achieve your goals for you and no one else. Are you aiming for this goal because you feel you 'should'? Are your end results truly favourable for you and anyone else involved?

Is Your End Result Compelling?

Whilst checking if your end results are favourable for you, it is also worth checking whether you want them enough. List several reasons for why you want to achieve each goal.

Do You Think You Deserve this goal?

Do you have any niggling gremlins over your 'right' to achieve this goal, or do you think you are 'unworthy' of it? If so, you may be better off working on your self worth before focusing on the goal. Do you think you need 'permission' to achieve the goal or the end result? Again, it may be worth you addressing these gremlins first.

Are Others Holding You Back?

Are the people in your life sapping your motivation? Maybe they are making you feel guilty for wanting to change or improve something?

Sometimes other people feel threatened or unsettled by change; they feel they may be 'left behind'. It's worth talking to everyone involved to clarify what you are hoping to achieve and how it benefits them all. If necessary, you may need to reassess your relationships with these people.

Recap So Far

So let's recap on what we have covered so far, in the Moving Forward chapters. We've covered those things we need to remember when working on our action plans – things such as taking ownership and making the decision to improve our current situation. We have also looked at how to set proper goals that are achievable and realistic. We have also looked at keeping motivated, along with those things that may negatively impact our motivation.

We know that we want to move forward by working on improving your confidence and esteem. More importantly, we now know that we can make the decision to work on our confidence and esteem, AND know that we can start from anywhere – without the need of any special tools, equipment or timings. So our next step is to get our action plan in place!

*"No one can persuade another to change. Each of us guards a gate of change
that can only be opened from the inside. We cannot open the gate of another,
either by argument or emotional appeal."*

– Marilyn Ferguson

CHAPTER 20

"Without change, something sleeps inside us, and seldom awakens. The sleeper must awaken."

– Frank Herbert

ACTION STATIONS!
Compiling your Action Plan

Whether you walk everywhere or drive, you already know your starting position and, you will know when you set out, that you need to know where you are headed! You can argue that you 'just go out for a walk or drive' but you still know both your starting position and that your ultimate end destination is – well, home!

It's the same with improving your self confidence and self esteem. You know you are starting in your current position, and you know what that means for you (as you have your list of those areas you want to work on from Sections 1 and 2), along with the benefits you gain from staying put (from Chapter 18), so you now need to know your end destination. You know, broadly speaking, that your end destination is 'improved confidence and/or esteem' but each individual is unique, so this end destination will look, and mean, different things for different people.

Tip:
Remember, you can make these 'Moving Forward' sections easier to complete, by grabbing your notepad and pen and taking your time answering the following.

Starting Position
Earlier in Section 2, I asked you to write down your comments and emotions relating to your current situation and your thoughts and feelings about you. If you haven't yet done that, re-visit this section and do so now. You should also have a list of benefits for staying as you are, as well as details of your stresses, emotions, fears, beliefs and self talk – again, you will need your answers for this section.

I also want you to answer the following questions:

- What do you need to do more of?
- What do you feel you 'should' do, or you 'aught' to do?
- What do you need to do less of?
- What do you need to stop doing?
- Who are those people who drag you down?

Go through all you have written about your current situation and circle any negative words used. Look for words such as:

- Powerless
- Unattractive
- Too busy
- Empty
- Lost
- No time
- Unhappy
- Annoyed

- Critical
- Without
- Scared

So now you are aware of where you currently are, we need to look at where you want to be.

How You Want To Be

I now want you write a few paragraphs in answer to each of the following again, but this time I want you to describe the person you want to be:

- appearance
- positive and negative thoughts about you
- likes and dislikes
- talents and character traits
- what you are scared of
- what you worry about
- what you dream about

Describe How You Interact With Other People

- How do other people talk to you?
- What friendship groups do you have
- What are the people you hang around with like? (Socially and in the work environment)

Describe Your 'Day in a Life'

Allow yourself to dream and run through an overview of an average day in your new life. Where you are, what you are wearing, what you do as well as how you act and interest with yourself and others. This is the 'end destination' you want to reach – so make it vibrant and exciting by introducing as many of your senses as you can! Also describe the following:

- Your relationship with your partner and/or children
- Your career
- Leisure and pleasure

List The Differences

Take a piece of paper and, on the left-hand side I want you to list your categories. Use the areas of your life from Section 2 as a guideline, but also add the extra categories:

- self confidence
- self esteem
- your appearance and mannerisms

Next to the categories write your end results. Then opposite what you have written, write how you would currently describe these areas.

Brainstorm

I now want you to take a big sheet of paper and brainstorm all your ideas for getting from where you are currently to having that new image of you and your life. Be as creative as you like and do not stop to think about the realities or technicalities of your ideas.

Circle those ideas that appeal to you the most, or sit the best with you.

Steps Forward

Now, taking those ideas that appealed the most, write down the steps you can take to get from your current position to the end destination. Break them down into small manageable chunks (this will vary depending on your goals) and add these steps to your Action Plan.

You will have two types of steps, and they are explained below.

Direct Steps

Direct steps are the ones you can list as a direct result of looking at your end destination. These include things like:

- Buy Chanel No.5 perfume (or get a sample of it)
- Wear something red more often (to match what you were wearing in your end destination)
- Make eye contact and smile at everyone I encounter
- Go out to a cafe or restaurant for tea and/or lunch once a week/month
- Hold my head up and my shoulder back when walking and standing
- Smile at myself in the mirror every day, then tell myself I am wonderful
- Get a travel brochure for Tuscany

Some of these steps are directly related to your appearance so, before you start screaming that confidence and esteem aren't directly related to your looks, I want you to see it a different way.

You are taking steps to become the person in your end destination. That involves not only how that confident you acted, but how you looked too. The chances are the confident you looked different too – even if she wore different shoes or wore her hair in a different style. For example, when you smell your new perfume, I want you to remember that confident you. When you look at the new hairstyle you have, I want you to remember that confident you. All these things will serve as reminders of your end destination.

Indirect Steps

These are the steps you need to take after looking at both your start and end destinations. After assessing both your starting and end positions, certain things (and people) will become apparent to you. These are things (and people) that need to be changed or eliminated from your life, as they are doing you no favours. These can quite often be broken down into even smaller steps. These indirect steps can include things such as:

- End contact with x,y,z (those 'friends' currently in your life who drag you down)
- Limit contact to once a week/month (select a suitable timescale)
- Let phone calls go to voicemail & call back when I'm ready to talk to them
- Keep contact to under 5 minutes (select suitable timescale for you)
- Talk to my partner about how he speaks to me
- Start saying 'no' to those requests I do not want to do

These actions may even give those 'friends' an opportunity to change their behaviour or drift away of their own accord – either way, it's good for you.

Timescales
Now go through your action steps and allocate a time period for completing them. If you need extra resources, finances or help make sure you allow time for them.

Check Your Action Plan

Now take your action plan steps and run them through the rules for setting goals (Chapter 19). If they pass, then great! If not, edit them as necessary and then re-check them. You now have a workable, individual action plan!

Dealing With The Gremlins

We look at gremlins that may arise in the next chapter, however for the purposes of your action plan I want you to relook at your ideal situation and, for each area of your life I want you to answer the following question:

- List all the reasons why you currently do not have this in your life

For example, you may have listed a loving, supportive partner, a bank account with lots of savings and a dress size two smaller than you currently are. Your reasons for not having these in your life could be obvious, such as: lack of money or easier to eat unhealthily as that's what is currently in your fridge. Less obvious answers could involve: others make fun of my exercising habits, I spend my money on things to make me happy and my partner makes me feel inadequate and inferior.

This will give you a list of underlying gremlins that may hinder your efforts. So use the following chapter as a resource for dealing with each of them.

*"Thinking you can achieve your goals without decisive action, is like
thinking you can win the lottery without buying a ticket."*

– Gary Ryan Blair

CHAPTER 21

*"The price of success is hard work, dedication to the job at hand,
and the determination that whether we win or lose,
we have applied the best of ourselves to the task at hand."*

– Vince Lombardi

SORTING THOSE GREMLINS THAT MAY HOLD YOU BACK

How To Change Your Beliefs

As our beliefs are rooted in our subconscious, it is easy to take it for granted that you are 'just the way you are' or 'this is the reality of who I am'. This is you justifying your beliefs and actions. Taking time to stop and think about what exactly your beliefs and values are is essential to ensure you get rid of any that aren't serving you, enabling you to live at your full potential. For the purposes of this book we are examining those related to you, your personality, work and home environment and your immediate surroundings, although the following pointers are just as useful for any other beliefs you may have.

Challenge your beliefs

Ask yourself where (and who) your beliefs originated from and if they are guiding you to live your life the way you want to live it. Write a list of all the statements that you currently have about yourself and your environment.

Decide which beliefs you want to keep – and which to replace

Some of your beliefs are to be kept, so decide which ones empower you; which ones make you feel good or positive. Any beliefs that make you feel heavy, sad, and miserable or any other negative feeling are the ones you need to replace.

Eliminate authority voices

Those beliefs you find that are linked to other people (or that use other people as the source of the belief need to be eliminated. When a belief is linked back to a person, decide whether that person has always been honest with their opinion, or if there have been times where they have been wrong. Then you have to decide how much authority you link to that person – would you trust them 100%, are they never ever wrong?

Take back control

Look for circumstances where you are feeling guilt or second-guessing another person. These are sure signs you have handed them control of your life and now it's not sitting right with you. Look for ways to take back that authority by finding the facts, rather than acting on the emotion. Remember, quite often it isn't **how** the other person is treating you – it is **how you feel about your view** of their treatment.

You can change your beliefs at any time

You make your own rules and beliefs to live by; waiting for everyone you encounter to accept you isn't going to happen – especially as they are all seeking acceptance as well. Learning to accept yourself and taking control of your life, beliefs and

How To Change Your Thoughts

As already discussed, words create our emotions, actions, our beliefs and how we form our lives. Therefore, these can also all be changed with words. Mastering your dialogue (especially internal dialogue) is the key to mastering your experience of life. So start by following the points below.

Notice Your Thoughts

To give you an idea of the wording used, spend the next 24 hours noticing the thoughts that run through your head. Most people are shocked by the amount of negativity coming from their subconscious mind.

Whose Voice Is It?

Not all negative inner talk is our own. When spending time noticing your thoughts, actually make a note of those phrases that are linked to another person, or those phrases you hear spoken in another person's voice. You can then analyse them to see if they are shaping any of the negative beliefs you may have. (see Chapter 13 for more on beliefs)

Enhance Your Vocabulary

Rather than using 'OK', 'fine' or 'good' to describe positive experiences, as they can diminish and flatten the feelings and emotions you have., evaluate them and choose a more descriptive word or sentence. 'I feel fantastic', 'I had an amazing day' and 'I loved doing/seeing...' all feel stronger and more emotional. Don't take my word for it – read this paragraph out loud and see how different these words feel to 'OK' 'fine' and good'!

Drop The Intensity of Negative Words

Following on from the previous point of enhancing positive wording; look to change the intensity of the negative words you use. 'Hate' is a strong emotional word, so drop the intensity and change it to 'I dislike' or better still 'I prefer'.

Stop Globalising

When faced with a challenging situation what runs through your head? Is it 'why does this always happen to me?' or similar – if so, you are globalising (or exaggerating) the situation. Think back to when you were a teenager (or if you have teenage children listen to their vocabulary!). They are very quick to use globalising words such as 'always', 'never' and 'everyone'. These words are great for enhancing the emotions you are feeling when speaking them.

Change Your Viewpoint

Rather than focusing on the negatives of a situation, look to focus on the positives. I don't mean pretend that the negative isn't happening by not talking about it or telling yourself that everything is rosy; but look for ways to voice them in a more positive way. For example change 'failing' to 'learning'; 'overwhelmed' to 'busy, 'rejected' to 'overlooked' and even 'depressed' to 'not on top of it'.

Change The Tone and Pictures

Athletes use pictures (visualisation) to motivate themselves and to see themselves performing perfectly. Authors (such as Stephen King) use the tone of their self talk to order themselves to write. Play around with the tone and pictures you associate with your self talk and see if it makes a difference to you. Maybe change the tone of negative self talk to that of Mickey Mouse or picture him wagging his finger at you rather than your mother or father. Have some fun with this one!

Stop Having Bad Days!

Telling yourself you are going to have a bad day, is a sure fire way to have one. So you may have gotten up late, your baby may have vomited their breakfast over you or the dog may have chewed a hole in your favourite shoes – but they are bad events; not a sign that the rest of your day is going to be just as bad. Turn it around and tell yourself 'things are looking up' and visualise the rest of your day going smoothly.

This applies to others who are having a bad day and think you should too. If you feel guilty or sad for them, you are only going to let their bad mood rub off on you. Decide now that you are the only person who gets to decide how your day is going to be. You do not have to get involved in their negativity and drama. If your child is throwing a temper tantrum on the floor, you know the quickest way to stop them is withdraw your attention. This also applies to adults who try to draw you into their bad mood!

Change Your Actions

As stated earlier in this chapter, your thoughts and words create your beliefs and actions. If you consciously change your actions you will be able to start changing your beliefs – and eventually you will change your negative self talk with more motivating phrases.

For example if you procrastinate, your new action would be to have a plan and to force yourself to work on the steps within that plan. Whilst working on them, you will feel better, more motivated and feel like you are achieving something. If done often enough, this will make you reassess your negative beliefs about your motivation and procrastination, so you will find more appropriate, positive beliefs to replace them with –

How To Get A Handle On Your Emotions

Put Them into A Positive Perspective

We sometimes find that past emotions are linked in negativity. If this is the case, you need to turn reinterpret them into a positive link. You can do this by taking the time to step back from the feeling and situation and reassessing it. Look for the gift or positive lesson learnt, for example you may have become a stronger or more determined person as a result of that situation. You want to reprogram your mind and cut off the painful link with this situation.

Take Responsibility

Believing you are helpless and have no power in your life is allowing you to stay in a 'self-pity' state of mind – it also relieves you of any responsibility for your life and your actions Stop blaming other people and stop living with a 'poor me' victim mentality. How you react and feel is down to how **you** interpret things – other people cannot **make** you react or feel a certain way. You have a choice as to how you interpret was others say and do. Decide now to take charge. Take control of **your** life and consciously create a life you deserve. Life doesn't just 'happen' to you – you are responsible for 'creating' what happens to you. If you don't like what you've been dealt – look at changing it.

Nip 'Guilt Trip's in the Bud

Learn to spot the signs of those people who like to try and make you feel guilty. This will enable you to nip it in the bud, before it gets out of hand. Learning to say 'no' – and then sticking to your decision is a valuable asset in your arsenal.

Next time someone is trying to jump on the guilt trip bandwagon, be firm in your decision and remind yourself: regardless of what they say, you are a worthwhile person who can make your own decisions.

Learn to Forgive

I know that this is a hard one to swallow if someone hurt you (physically or mentally) or treated you wrongly, but forgiving them will enable you to move forward with your life. Holding onto the hurt and anger is not affecting them in any way, shape or form – but it is hurting you. Feeling strong negative feelings and emotions for any length of time will keep you stuck; whilst weighing down on your mind and soul – not to mention the negative effects it can have on your health.

Take the time to talk to someone or get your thoughts down on paper. I found writing a letter to the person helps a lot. You don't have to send it – I burnt mine in the back garden, then stood and watched the flames and smoke take my pain away – it was quite liberating!

Listen to Your Emotions

Learning to read the information your body sends to you will build a better connection between your body and mind; and your inner soul. Your emotions are sending you vital information that should be listened to and dealt with – they are drawing your attention to something – and avoiding them will frequently lead to pain and unhappiness.

Taking the time to read and understand your body's reaction to things will lead you to inner fulfilment and a deeper sense of peace – with yourself and others. So next time you are having an emotional reaction to something, take a step back and assess why you are reacting the way you are and look for the lessons. Are you reacting to the actual event/situation or actually reacting to a past one? Are your reactions justified or are you overreacting? Are you reacting to what was said – or how you are interpreting it?

Practice Gratitude

Notice all the good things and blessing around you. Practice saying 'thank you'; not only when someone helps you but when something good happens generally. Keep a 'gratitude journal' and each day write down 5-10 things you are grateful for – these can be helpful things someone has done for you, positive comments, how well the children have behaved or even the weather! Like attracts like – so focusing on good things will make you more aware of other good things in your life.

Know What Makes You Happy

All too often we find it easier to voice what we don't like; those things that make us sad, mad and unhappy. Knowing what makes us happy seems to be a bit harder, so take the time to notice who and what makes you happy. Whether you like curling up with a good book or watching an old black and white film, make a note of those things that make you smile. Next time you are having a bad day, make an effort to pull yourself into a better mood by doing something that makes you happy – after all, you can change your emotions and feelings any time you wish.

How To Manage Stress

The biggest step when dealing with stress is to identify the actual cause of it. To help you identify the causes, spend time noticing how you feel and react to situations, events, people and places in your life. Once identified, there are several things you can do to combat stress.

Breathing Exercises

These exercises can regulate your mood, reduce your stress levels and leave you feeling energised. Become aware of your breathing pattern and ensure you spend time practising exhaling completely, letting all the air out of your lungs and taking nice deep, slow breaths in. Get into the habit of making time to take a slow deep breath in and out, before answering a question or making a decision – this gives you time to connect with your body and relax enough to ensure your decision is right for you. Learning to meditate and/or using visualisation techniques are also good ways of focusing your breathing, whilst unwinding and releasing tension.

Exercise

If done regularly, this is great for reducing stress, easing tension and promoting relaxation. This may mean simply walking more, rather than using your car or putting a bit more energy into household chores. Aerobic exercise particularly, will help you moderate the effect stress has on your emotions. Exercise also has the ability to lift you from a bad or low mood, whilst yoga (or other stretching exercises) will help you tone your body, aid relaxation and help you learn to breathe properly.

Think Positively!

Expressing your positive emotions and being optimistic has a range of health benefits; including lowering your production of cortisol, boosting your immune function and reducing the risk of chronic diseases.

Manage Your Eating & Sleeping Patterns

Ensure you are eating a healthy diet and ensure you are not having too much caffeine, sugar or alcohol. It is essential that you get an adequate amount of sleep, so establish a bedtime routine for yourself that will enable you to wind down before settling down to sleep. Remember, sleep allows your body to have time to repair and rejuvenate – so get into the habit of having a set 'lights out' time!

Talk!

Finding a good friend or trusted relative who you can confide in will enable you to voice your concerns and worries. All too often we find it easier to bottle things inside – those things that annoy us, upset us and stress us out. It is essential that you do not bottle up your emotions – so you can effectively, an honestly, deal with those things that are bothering you. Often, just the process of talking something through, will enable you to see a solution that was otherwise hidden to you. It is also a good way of getting those things that annoy you off your chest – although make sure you keep it solution orientated, rather than turning into a rant!

Some people benefit from going to a support group and connecting with other people in their situation (mother and toddler groups, women's networking groups, groups related to particular hobbies etc). Take your time to check out all the options in your area, as you want to make sure both the people and environment are a right fit for you.

Prioritise

Evaluate your priorities. Take time out to work out those things in your life that are important to you – and look at limiting or ridding yourself of those things that aren't. Part of this is actually learning your limitations – both personal (your abilities) and time related. Sometimes, learning to say 'no' may be hard, but will make you a happier person.

Learn to Adapt

Learning to adapt to different situations will enable you to take control of them. Adapting to suit circumstances can include leaving earlier to avoid traffic, changing your parenting techniques or establishing firm and consistent guidelines for your children or changing your routine to ensure you have some time to relax and unwind. Maybe there are things you currently have in your routine that can be passed to your partner or child? We are all guilty of trying to be superwoman buy adapting can sometimes mean trusting others to take some of the chores (and weight) off your shoulders.

Learn to Balance Your Time & Energy

Women especially, have to juggle many different roles. Whether you are a wife, mother, career woman or stay at home mum, too much of any one role will cause stress in your life. Running around after everyone else seems to be imbedded in us the minute we marry and have children. It is therefore important to find the right balance between them all.

Ensure you take a few moments, on a regular basis, to relieve your stress levels. Simply walking, stretching and having a few minutes on your own or in the fresh air, is enough to help lower your stress levels. If you're one of these people (I know, I was one!) who has a bath in 5 minutes and has the pets and/or children in with you when you use the bathroom – stop! Reaffirm your boundaries; turn bath time into your time and allow yourself precious moments to gather your thoughts and have a bit of breathing space – for the sake of your sanity!

If you're home all day with the children, organise regular time out on your own, to pursue a hobby, take up a course or just have a coffee in a local cafe whilst reading a good book. It is also important that you have regular one-on-one time with those important people in your life – your partner, friends, children – so organise special time for them on a weekly or monthly basis. You are more inclined to stay calm and focused if you have control of your time and plan your use of it wisely.

Plan and prepare things in advance to ensure you have all the necessary things to hand when needed, for both work related and home related things. Writing shopping lists for the week ahead may seem pointless, however it will save you precious time (and money!) when you visit the supermarket.

Live in The Now

Focus your attention on the present moment and the job at hand. Whether that is work-related or having a conversation with someone, focusing on what you are doing will lead to less errors and reduced anxiety and tension. This includes learning to be patient. If you are sat in a traffic jam, getting stressed really isn't going to help the situation or your blood pressure.

Learning to deal with what is in the present moment, rather than stressing about future possibilities and events will pay wonders with your stress and anxiety levels. Look for the hidden gifts in every situation and practice being grateful for everything you have.

Have a Laugh and Enjoy Yourself!

Increase your sense of humour and increase the endorphins in your body. These are the chemicals released in your body when you're happy – they also help to boost your immune system – so put something funny on the TV and laugh your socks off!

Giving yourself permission to indulge yourself reaffirms your self worth and allows you to enjoy yourself. Indulging in a movie, music, massage, hair cut or even a book is a good way of taking some enjoyment time just for you to unwind and relax.

Have a Goal

Having a definite goal to achieve gives you a sense of purpose and helps focus your mind. When things get tough or go wrong in your daily life, knowing you are striving towards your dreams and goals will help relieve some of that stress and frustration and leave you feeling less 'stuck'. Planning your goal and breaking it down into steps will highlight how achievable it is for you and will also allow you to feel less stress by any changes ahead.

How To Solve Your Fears

Managing fear and worry will take hard work, so be patient with yourself and stay committed to solving your problem. Worrying about something will not change anything – and remember that most of what you worry about never comes true anyway!

It is also worth pointing out that avoiding your problem through the use of alcohol or illegal drugs will not solve the problem in the long run. You will still have the problem you started with – unless you face it head on and deal with it. So, concentrate on what you are able to do and focus on solving this fear or worry.

Find The Source

This is the main seed of your particular fear. Peel back the layers of your fear to find the real underlying source. You may think you just have a fear of spiders – but why? Keep asking yourself 'why?' until you have the real reason. That fear of spiders will have a root cause. It may be a fear of dying (snake venom, stories told about killer spiders, seen someone bitten and subsequently died) or a fear of being violated (spider getting inside you, laying eggs or harming your body in some way). So ask yourself questions such as:

- Why am I afraid?
- What am I afraid will happen?
- What is causing this anxiety?
- What do I associate with this event/situation/object etc?
- What evidence do I have and what are the facts?
- What weight does that evidence have?

You may find it easier to brainstorm and write down anything you associate with this fear – feelings, emotions, images, events etc. If the words of a person had an influence on you having this fear – how much weight do you give that person? Are they usually trustworthy and honest? Do you value this person or do they not actually mean that much to you?

Find A Solution

Look for ways to solve this fear. Brainstorm possible techniques and solutions that can help. For example, you may have a fear of speaking your mind, being assertive or public speaking. The solution may be to join your local Toastmasters group. That way, you'll learn how to speak clearly and succinctly in front of other people.

The solution may be to find proof that this fear is wrong or incorrect. For example, in a fear of flying you could look into the facts of aeroplane and flight, the statistics of flying safety versus car safety etc.

Change Your Thinking

A good way to manage a fear or worry is to replace the negative thoughts with positive ones. When you feel anxious, ask yourself questions that will maintain your objectivity and common sense. Counteract a negative thought with facts – relate to past events or occurrences where you were in the same situation but survived it and were fine as a result.

A good way to change your thinking is to actually have facts relating to the situation. Gathering facts can stop us making exaggerated or fearful assumptions, whilst keeping us focused on the reality of the situation we are in.

Some people find it beneficial to have a phrase (or affirmation) or a particular song that makes them feel safe and happy. If so, replace the negative thoughts with this.

The Perfect Time is Now!

Waiting until the time is right will ensure you have a very long wait. You can argue that you are waiting for more information, more time, a less busy time, when the kids are asleep etc, etc, but there will never be a better time to deal with a fear than now. If you keep waiting – you will never get rid of that fear. This leads onto the next solution...

Take Some Form of Action!

Break down the solution into smaller steps. I'm not suggesting you go and hug a Tarantula if you have a fear of spiders – make that your end step! In the meantime, make a list of smaller, easier to achieve steps towards your end solution. Maybe being in the same room as a spider in a tank is a big achievement for you – so set this up as one of your steps.

If you worry about letting people down, maybe have saying 'no' to one request as your first step. By completing small steps every day, you can bring a solution that much closer to you, whilst minimising the stress to a more manageable level. This is made so much easier if you actually have a plan to follow (as per Section 3!).

Deal With The Emotions

Whilst taking steps to cure a fear it is perfectly natural that you will get up upset. The important thing to remember is to keep this within a manageable level. If that means backing off slightly, to enable you to get a bit calmer, then do it. If you push too hard you will make the fear even bigger. The point I am trying to make is that you **keep stress to a manageable level**.

I'm not saying that you give up on the step you are trying to achieve but to have a safe enough distance to allow yourself to calm down. Using the earlier example, if you want to be able to walk into a room that houses a spider tank, but you get too shaky and upset – go to a safer, less threatening distance until you have calmed down – **then try again**. You can repeat this until you have succeeded.

Get Advice and Advice If Needed

If you uncover something you really aren't sure how to deal with, consult with a health professional – either a GP or therapist. Sometimes talking it over with a professional will help make finding a solution easier.

"Where you are headed is more important that now fast you are going.
Rather than always focusing on what's urgent,
learn to focus on what is really important."

– Stephen Covey

SECTION 4 – TOOLS IN YOUR ARSENAL

This section lists all those tools that can help you to stay motivated, positive and moving forward, whilst working on your action plan. These tools are also useful once you have finished achieving all the steps in your action plan, as they will help you keep your newly improved confidence and esteem.

CHAPTER 22

*"We either make ourselves miserable, or we make ourselves strong.
The amount of work is the same."*

– Carlos Castaneda

AFFIRMATIONS & POSITIVITY QUOTES

What is an Affirmation?

An affirmation is its simplest form is a statement that you repeat over and over. For the purposes of self development, it is a positive statement that you consciously repeat over and over to yourself. Note the use of the words 'positive' and 'consciously' – as already explained, a lot of our self talk is currently negative and subconscious – and for self development reasons we want to empower ourselves and move forward.

A lot of the points made in the previous section on self talk, stress the importance of noticing (or being conscious) of the wording we use. Affirmations are positive phrases we can use to replace those negative thoughts we have noticed. Conscious repetition of these positive phrases will, in time, lead them to create more positive, empowering pathways in our subconscious mind.

How To Use Affirmations

You can create your own affirmations easily. Grab a few quiet minutes to write down your current negative thoughts. Now write down the opposite of them, for example 'I am a useless person' becomes 'I am a worthwhile person'. You can select one or two to focus on first and move on to others whenever you feel the need to change them, however it is worth remembering that it takes approximately 21 days to replace a negative thought; so you want to aim for this timescale on each one. To ensure their effectiveness there are however, a few guidelines to using affirmations and they are as follows:

Keep in the Positive

Obviously you want to keep the affirmation positive, so make sure you use positive wording. This also includes avoiding double negatives such as 'I am no longer...' becomes 'I am...' or 'I am now...' Using 'thank you' is another winner, as using gratitude will open us up to being willing to receive what we are asking for.

Use Present Tense

Your affirmations must be voiced in present tense, so use the word 'now' rather than 'I will become...' or 'one day I will...'

Pump up the Emotion

Linking a good feeling to your affirmation will ensure you see a faster, positive change. The more intense the feeling – the faster the change.

Commit to Memory

The final step is to repeat your affirmation so often that your believe it and it becomes rooted in your subconscious. You can make this easier on yourself by placing your affirmations somewhere prominent; your bathroom mirror, on your fridge, or on a small card in your pocket. You want to be able to refer to them throughout your day.

That's the 'memory' part of this step dealt with; we now need to address 'commit'. Commit to putting your full efforts into this for the next 90 days. They say it takes 21 days to make something a habit – allowing 90 will ensure it is rooted in your subconscious. After all, you have nothing to lose – and so much to gain.

What are positivity quotes and what are they used for?

Positivity quotes are those little quotes that make you feel happy, positive and allow you to reflect on their content. They can be inspiring or thought-provoking too. They serve a similar purpose to affirmations – to keep you motivated and inspired throughout your day. The main difference though is affirmations are phrases you write to suit your needs and wishes, whereas positivity quotes are usually written by someone else.

How to use positivity quotes

The best way to use quotes is to place them in prominent places, so you can see them throughout the day. Maybe you could place them next to your affirmations.

I usually print (or write) my affirmations and positive quotes on small pieces of card; that way you can carry them around with you in your pocket or purse. I have also printed out those quotes that inspire me the most, and then I've laminated them so I can display them in my office.

Another good tip is to get a small spiral bound notebook and write any new quotes you hear during your day-to-day routines (this also applies to anything that crops up that could be good for you as a new affirmation.

*"When we think positively and imagine what we want,
we risk disappointment;
when we don't, we ensure it."*

– Lana Limpert

CHAPTER 23

> *"Vision without action is merely a dream.*
> *Action without vision just passes the time.*
> *Vision with action can change the world."*
>
> – Joel Barker

VISUALISATION & VISION BOARDS

What is visualisation?

Simply put, visualisation is the pictures you have in your mind, similar to when you are dreaming; however with visualisation you are awake. Your brain doesn't actually know the difference between something you have vividly imagined and something you have actually done, so this means you can 'trick' your brain into thinking it has already achieved something. Why would you want to do this? Well if your mind believes the outcome is already a successfully completed one – it believes it will be easy to achieve the same result again. Sportsmen and women have been using visualisation for years to imagine already running and winning a race or event they are about to enter.

Motivation and visualisation

Motivation is great for propelling you forward towards a goal; however visualisation is like rocket fuel for your motivation. It provides you with a clear blueprint for what you want to be motivated towards. As we all know, trying to succeed without having any idea (or vision) of where you are going will lead you to going round in circles and getting nowhere fast. You will end up frustrated, disappointed and disillusioned.

How to use visualisation

Now you know what visualisation is, as well as how it can work, it is time to look at how you can implement it in your life.

Picture your end result

Look at what you want to achieve. It could be a job promotion, new home, lose a few pounds or a tidy home. Visualise it as a moving scene – so see yourself in your home or in your new job or environment, looking at the things around you. See it through your eyes whilst you are in that scene, rather than from a spectator's view of watching you from a distance in that scene. Are there other people around you – if so, who? Where are you? What do you see around you? What are you wearing? Notice your posture and attitude, how you hold your posture and how you interact with others. Picture it as vividly as you can.

Add your senses and emotions

Make your visualisation alive by adding emotion and using all your senses. What do you smell? How do you feel? Do you feel pride, love, success, happiness? Where do you feel that emotion (in your chest, heart, all over your body)? Are you eating exotic or different foods – if so, how does it taste and how does feel in your mouth? What do the materials around you feel like? Are they soft, heavy, rigid or fluid? Can you feel the breeze around you, smell the ocean or feel the rain on your face? Do you hear birds, cars, people? Engage all your senses and emotions.

Enhance it all further

Now ramp up the volume and adjust that brightness. Make the colours richer, the sounds louder and the emotion stronger. Radiate that emotion and feeling around your body. If you want to picture it as a colour, do so and radiate that colour from every pore of your body. *Really* feel yourself there, experiencing what you are experiencing.

Act 'as if'

You've heard of the saying 'fake it until you make it'; well apply that to your visualisation. Act as if you have already achieved it. If your posture was different or you acted differently; copy it in your current situation. If you wore certain materials or smelt certain aromas; bring something that reminds you of it into your current situation. If you dressed differently or wore your hair differently then start bringing those changes to life. Ok, you might have been driving a Ferrari or Aston Martin that would make it impossible to get now (let alone fit the baby car seat in!) but there's nothing to stop you reliving your feelings and emotions whilst you're driving your current model!

Visit frequently

Being a frequent flyer means you collect rewards – the same applies to your vision. The more you visualise it, the more connected you will be to it; and the more you will benefit in the long run. Repeating your visualisation frequently will ensure you imbed your desired end result in your mind – and the more likely your mind will help find ways to achieve it.

Watch your language

When talking and discussing your future goals and ambitions be sure to keep it in a positive, upbeat tone and use positive language. Talk in terms of 'when I' rather than 'if I' and 'I will' rather than 'I might'.

Cherish your vision

Treat your vision as special to you. Be careful who you share it with, as there will be people who would take pleasure in laughing at your aspirations or questioning your abilities. If you find someone who you wish to share it with, make sure they will encourage and help you, rather than judge and belittle you.

Get motivated

As mentioned at the start of this section, your visualisation goes hand-in-hand with motivation, so use this as a starting point for getting motivated and actually getting into action. You don't have to necessarily know *how* you will achieve all the things you visualise, however you can add things to your action plan that you can do and start taking steps towards what you want to achieve.

What are vision boards?

Vision boards are an extension or follow-on from basic visualisation. They are a visual reference of all you want to achieve and also act as a stimulus for your goals. They provide a creative way of referencing the visual, emotive and sensory material seen in your visualisation, as well as other things you would one day like to have or achieve.

How do you create and use vision boards?

Vision boards are easy to create and simple to use. Start collecting anything that relates to your visualisation, your goals or ambitions. You can go through magazines and cut out pictures of those things you would like to have or experience (for example, cars or trips), you can cut out places you'd like to visit and people you'd like to meet.

It is also a good idea to collect pictures of people showing those emotions you want to feel. For example you could have pictures of loving couples, happy families, smiling faces or people jumping for joy.

I've put pictures of houses I'd like to live in and leaflets for places I'd like to visit on my vision board, as well as pictures of people. Emotions and even money and bank statements with extra zeros on them! Look for words that inspire you and cut them out too. And you don't have to limit yourself to one board – you could have one for each of your goals!

Don't just limit yourself to pictures – get creative! Use dried flowers, napkins from restaurants and you can even have small objects that are relevant to you and your visualisation. You can use a plain corkboard to display your pictures, or cover a thick piece of card or wood.

"When your vision is simple and clear, you attract those ready to work with you.
A vision is less about the future – more about today.
Because a person with a vision already acts as if the vision lives in the present moment.
It's merely a matter of time, not if."

– Thomas Leonard

CHAPTER 24

"Gratitude unlocks the fullness of life. It turns what we have into enough, and more. It turns denial into acceptance, chaos to order, confusion to clarity. It can turn a meal into a feast, a house into a home, a stranger into a friend. Gratitude makes sense of our past, brings peace for today, and creates a vision for tomorrow."

– Melody Beattie

GRATITUDE & GRATITUDE JOURNALS

What is Gratitude?

Gratitude is the state of being grateful; being thankful for something. It is easy to go through life focusing on the negativity around us; the people who annoy us, the queues and traffic jams, the bad mood our partner/children/friends are in, but this pulls us down, leaving us feeling unhappy, stuck and depressed.

When we look at life as an opportunity; a way to grow and learn, a place to love, we open our minds and hearts to the good things around us; the blessings, the people who help and support us and the healing and peace this provides. This raises us, leaving us feeling uplifted, happy, content and happy.

Spend a few minutes remembering the last time you were grateful for something that happened; the last time you said 'thank you' and meant it – the last time you were grateful for being you.

Why use gratitude?

There are several benefits to actively using gratitude. It not only helps us feel better about ourselves and the world around us; it enables us to be in a better frame of mind and body. Gratitude is also a two-way street; it helps you focus on the positive in your life, plus it enables you to boost another person's self worth, when you praise them.

The positive side effects on our emotions and mood

Feeling positive emotions comforts and relaxes us, leaving us feeling:

- Positive
- Optimistic
- Motivated
- Fulfilled
- Focuses us on finding more to feel grateful for

The positive effects on our body

Gratitude also affects our physical body in different ways. These include:

- Enhancing the healing system in our body
- Stress hormone levels such as cortisol and norepinephrine decrease
- Your body is flooded with immune-boosting endorphins
- Blood levels increase to your heart as your arteries relax
- In turn, this raises the amount of oxygen your tissues receive

So how else does all this affect you? Well, just in case you needed further convincing, here are a few more reasons to be grateful!

Gratitude helps fight stress and depression

Gratitude gives you a natural 'high' and this not only increases your enthusiasm, alertness and determination; it also boosts your optimism and energy. This in turn helps you to feel less stressed and depressed. It helps you to do more to help alleviate stress and depression, as when feeling more enthusiastic and determined, you are more likely to start exercising and taking active steps towards achieving your personal goals.

Gratitude helps you deal more love and joy

This helps you to express sincere appreciation and love, providing an antidote to feelings of regret, envy, resentment and fear.

Gratitude helps you cope with day-to-day traumas

As mentioned above, gratitude helps you manage stress and stressful situations. This prevents us from seeing those day-to-day upsets and traumas as huge mountains in our path. It helps us to clarify what is important and minimise what isn't. It enables us to be less emotionally charged by negative events and accept them for what they are – just moments in time. Gratitude also installs a sense of equality and balance; we are more able to rationalise that good and bad events happen to everyone.

Gratitude expands

Practising gratitude allows us to express our love, gratitude and appreciation. It turns your focus to finding more things to appreciate and gives you a renewed sense of gratitude for the things you do have.

Things that stop you showing gratitude

The two biggest reasons why I believe people don't practice gratitude are as follows

Focusing on the negative

We all know how easy it is to get caught up in negativity around us; in our immediate circle, work-related and world-related. This unfortunately trains us to always be focusing on the negatives – and not noticing the positives.

Feeling unworthy of gratitude

Some people believe they are unworthy of being shown gratitude. This stems from having a low self worth; a low opinion of themselves along with having thoughts of having nothing to be grateful for.

Feeling you haven't done enough

It is easy to feel as if you haven't done enough to 'earn' yours (and other peoples) gratitude. You've completed a task or goal, but keep thinking of ways you could've improved or perfected it.

Using size to determine gratitude

Relating the size or enormity of the task to whether it deserves gratitude is a similar follow-on to the above point. We feel the task wasn't big enough to warrant any 'fuss'.

Ways to use gratitude in your life

Change your focus

Look for good things to focus on. Practise this easily by setting yourself a goal of finding 10 or 20 things a day to be grateful for – this can be things you have achieved, people you can thank and compliment or life in general.

Become aware

Notice when you are focusing on negative events and people. Train yourself to flip your focus back onto something positive, enabling you to gradually retrain your habits to more productive ones.

Look for the positive

In challenging situations make an extra effort to notice the gift or lesson you can learn from them. If a person is annoying you, look for something positive about them and their attitude that you can be thankful for. Maybe the fact they are annoying you enables you to see what you can work on in your own emotions or character? Alternatively, they could be highlighting how grateful you are to have a better handle on your feelings or temper?

Voice gratitude

Take the time to thank others for their help. Thank your partner, your children, your friends and extended family, the cashier, postman, delivery guy – and remember to thank yourself. You can be thankful you got through a challenging day, thankful for achieving a task you were putting off and even thankful for staying calm!

Be grateful for everything

It doesn't matter how big or small the achievement, or how insignificant or normal the event; be thankful for everything.

Use gratitude for what you will have

Using gratitude to help you focus on things you would like to experience or have, is similar to an affirmation. Saying it in the present tense, as if you already have it is important. It helps keep you focused and ensures your brain thinks it's easy to achieve – as it believes you already have. Write a letter to the Universe giving thanks for the wonderful family and live you are now living. Explain it in detail, describe an average day.

Gratitude journal

Keeping a gratitude journal can be a key part of living a happy and prosperous life. When you write down a list and acknowledge all those things and people you appreciate, you compile a visual reference that can be used as a reminder when you are feeling low. You can then use this as a positive tool to get you quickly out of an unhappy, ranting mode and back onto a happy, positive state of mind. This in turn, will ensure your focus is on the positive things in your life, rather than on the negative and those things you may currently lack.

The act of physically writing things down reinforces them in your subconscious, whilst allowing you to experience the positive feelings associated with gratitude; when you write and when you re-read what you have written.

Being grateful allows you to appreciate those things you would normally take for granted and allows you to appreciate those people who are no longer with you. So, how to use a gratitude journal?

How to use a gratitude journal

You can use a normal diary; just make sure you take the time to write in it every day. Here are some tips to get you started.

- Set yourself a set number of things to write every day (anything from 5 upwards)

- Get into the habit of giving yourself 5-10 minutes alone with your journal, at the end of each day, to record your items
- Set yourself prompts to get you started – for example, 'I am thankful for', 'I am happy that' and 'I appreciate'.
- Ensure everything is mentioned in a positive tone, so no 'I'm so glad I do not...' rather 'I'm so glad I am/do...'

"Be thankful for what you have; you'll end up having more.
If you concentrate on what you don't have, you will never, ever have enough."

– Oprah Winfrey

SUMMARY

I hope you now have your action plan in place, and will use it to make those small steps towards boosting your confidence and esteem.

In the section that follows, I have given you details of those books and websites that I found essential when I embarked on my own self improvement journey. I have also provided details of my new six week online course. I hope you will find these resources as useful in your journey as I did. You will also find my contact details in the following section – I'd love to hear how you are getting on, so please feel free to contact me with your success stories!

I Couldn't End This Book Without Saying A Big Thank You – To You:

Once again, I would like to thank you for purchasing this book and having the faith that you would find your answers within. I hope it has opened your eyes to the enormous amount of possibilities that are available to you, regardless of where you are from and how you currently live your life.

As I mentioned in the forward for this book, this book is an introduction into boosting your self confidence and self esteem. I hope it has given you a peek into the 'you' that is inside, the vibrant, confident, assured you that is eager to come up to the surface and commence living that fulfilled, enjoyable and wonderful life she yearns for.

My wish is for you to finish this book feeling inspired and motivated, with a workable action plan for you to follow, as you embark on the start of your journey toward improved self confidence and self esteem.

I would also love to help you more with your improved confidence and esteem journey. Further details of how I can help you further are included in the 'Further Help' section that follows.

I would also love to help you more with your improved confidence and esteem journey. Further details of how I can help you further are included in the 'Further Help' section that follows.

If you've enjoyed this book and found it has been of benefit to you, I'd be honoured if you could spare a minute or two to leave a quick review on Amazon. Simply go directly to this books sales page on Amazon via the short-links below, and click on the 'write a review' button:

Amazon.co.uk http://amzn.to/NkCw5u
Amazon.com http://amzn.to/P7aCZv

I hope you enjoy your journey towards improved self confidence and self esteem!

Sarah x

SECTION 5 – FURTHER HELP AND AVAILABLE RESOURCES

FURTHER HELP AND CONTACT INFORMATION

Books Worth Getting

How to do Everything and be Happy by Peter Jones
ISBN: 0956885608
Available in both paperback and kindle versions on Amazon:
http://tinyurl.com/Do-Everything-Be-Happy-Now

Happy For No Reason by Marci Shimoff
ISBN: 141654772X
Available in paperback, hardback and audio on Amazon:
http://tinyurl.com/Happiness-For-No-Reason

You Can Heal Your Life by Louise L Hay
ISBN: 0937611018
Available in paperback, audio and kindle on Amazon:
http://tinyurl.com/Heal-Your-Own-Life

Secrets About Life Every Woman Should Know by Barbara de Angelis
ISBN: 0007323689
Available in both paperback and audio on Amazon:
http://tinyurl.com/Secrets-About-Life-For-Women

Websites to Mark as Favourites

Gimundo:
   A free daily newsletter, filled with inspiration, happy news, videos and much more! Boost you happiness and

positivity daily!
http://gimundo.com/

Insight of the Day:
Start your day with a positive message to reflect upon. You'll receive a free daily positive quote (Monday – Thursday) and an inspiring story every Friday!
http://www.insightoftheday.com

Contacting The Author:
If you have any comments directly related to the composition and work within this book, or would like to contact the author about anything related to her work, please feel free to use the author contact details given below:

By email: **sarah@sarahpjwhite.com**
Website: **www.sarahpjwhite.com**

ABOUT THE AUTHOR

Sarah PJ White is a qualified life coach and alternative therapist, with a passion for helping women improve their self confidence and self esteem.

She is a keen amateur photographer and is also interested in gardening – this interest prompted her to write her first EBook entitled *The Little Book of Elder'*.

She is the author of numerous articles, reports, workbooks and courses for Self Confidence Workshops – a website she founded in 2011 to help adults improve their self confidence and self esteem (http://www.selfconfidenceworkshops.co.uk).

Sarah is currently writing her first two fiction novels – in the thriller and supernatural mystery genres and hopes to have them published during 2012/2013.

Sarah lives in Berkshire, England, with her husband, daughter and hyperactive rescue dog, Danny.

www.ingramcontent.com/pod-product-compliance
Lightning Source LLC
Chambersburg PA
CBHW051433290426
44109CB00016B/1543